CHARTER REFORM IN CHICAGO

Southern Illinois University Press
Carbondale and Edwardsville

Maureen A. Flanagan

CHARTER
REFORM
IN
CHICAGO

Copyright © 1987 by the Board of Trustees,
Southern Illinois University
All rights reserved
Printed in the United States of America
Edited by Yvonne D. Mattson
Designed by Cindy Small
Production supervised by Natalia Nadraga

90 89 88 87   4 3 2 1

Library of Congress Cataloging-in-Publication Data

Flanagan, Maureen A., 1948–
  Charter reform in Chicago.

  Revision of thesis (Ph. D.).
  Bibliography: p.
  Includes index.
  1. Chicago (Ill.)—Politics and government—
To 1950. 2. Chicago (Ill.)—Charters—History
20th century. I. Title.
JS708.F54 1987   320.8'09773'11   86–29696
ISBN 0–8093–1391–X

The paper used in this publication meets the minimum requirements
of American National Standard for Information Sciences
–Permanence of Paper for Printed Library Materials,
ANSI Z39.48-1984. ∞™

For Chip

CONTENTS

PREFACE

When, in graduate school, I decided to study cities in the Progressive Era, the framework for considering the political history of cities in that era was that of a struggle between two opposing camps. The city was the arena in which reformers fought against the corruption of old-style bosses. Within this framework, the crucial questions asked were who among urban residents were the reformers, exactly what reforms did they wish to implement, and why. In general, the answers found that the reformers were good government advocates seeking to eradicate machine politics by centralizing municipal governments into the hands of a few experts whose nonpartisanship would replace party patronage as the guiding principle of municipal government. The municipal charter reform movement of the Progressive Era was one of the important reform issues examined to arrive at these answers.

Having grown up in the Chicago of Richard J. Daley, I had always taken the existence of the Democratic machine rather for granted; and the terms *machine politics*, *political boss*, *reform candidate*, and *party patronage* were early a part of my vocabulary. Because so much was written about bosses and machine politics with political reform mentioned only in passing, I had also assumed that little political reform had been attempted in Chicago during the Progressive Era. Thus, Jane Addams' cryptic mention of a new municipal charter in her book *Twenty Years at Hull-House* both surprised and intrigued me. I set out to find out what had happened to charter reform in Chicago and par-

ticularly to find out why the reformers of Chicago had failed in
their task to reform Chicago's municipal government along the
lines being implemented in many other cities at the time.

Even before I had proceeded very far into my work, I was
skeptical of the reformers-versus-bosses approach. Historians
had discovered upper-class, old middle-class, new middle-class,
working-class, and even ethnic reformers; and each group was
seen as pursuing different reforms. With so many groups in
cities identified as reformers, the term itself no longer seemed to
tell us anything. Then, in the wealth of material available on
the charter movement in Chicago I found that rather than a
fight between party bosses and a group of reformers, the charter
movement was a contest among Chicagoans across all class, ethnic, and gender lines to redefine good municipal government.
Few of the city's residents opposed charter reform, but they vehemently disagreed about how to accomplish it and how a new
charter should reorder the government. Behind their conflicting
ideas lay different visions of how the city as a whole should work
and to what purposes.

I also discovered the timeliness of the charter reform movement in Chicago's contemporary political scene. The current
struggle between the mayor and the city council for control of
the municipal government, for instance, is possible because
there is still no locus of power in the city. The political structure
was never formally centralized, and, as a result, power rests
with whatever faction controls the most votes in the council.
When there is no clear-cut majority or when the Mayor does not
control enough votes, the result is municipal chaos. The con-
fusion over terminology has not ceased either. Mayor Harold
Washington is categorized as a reformer or as a machine politician depending on who is doing the categorizing.

The dissertation I set out to write about a failed reform
movement ultimately turned into this book about the charter reform movement as an integral piece of Chicago's political history. The reasons for the movement's failure lay deeply em-
bedded in the city's history and its political culture, in which the
struggle over charter reform was part of a continual struggle to
determine municipal priorities among people who differed over

what these should be. In Chicago's charter movement, I found that the past experiences of Chicagoans in their earlier struggles over municipal issues had shaped their views about good urban government and helped determine their ideas about good charter reform. Because they did not agree on either of these issues, they could not compromise, and they eventually rejected the new municipal charter as written.

The failure of Chicago's charter reform movement in turn helped produce the conditions for the consolidation and endurance of the political machine later in the century. Left with an old-style decentralized municipal structure that could not cope adequately with the needs of a rapidly growing twentieth-century industrial city, Chicagoans had to find other ways to reorder their political environment. The Democratic machine would become the eventual compromise.

During my work on this book, several scholars have been particularly helpful. Thomas Kelly introduced me to the study of urban history and Chicago history and started me on the path to this book several years ago. His work came full circle with the invaluable suggestions he gave me on this manuscript. Lewis Erenberg has given help and advice since this project began; he read parts of the manuscript in various stages, and from him came the suggestion to think about the political culture of cities. Henry Binford has offered constant encouragement and shared his always thoughtful ideas on urban history with me. Several years of discussion with Harold Platt helped push me toward my analysis of urban history in the Progressive Era, and Paul Green's comments on an earlier version of this manuscript sharpened the ideas and arguments of the revision. I wish to thank them all.

Robyn Muncy contributed in a different way to this book. She took valuable time from her own dissertation research to collect vital materials and send them to me when I was several thousand miles away from my sources. Her willingness to do this and her thoroughness contributed much to chapter 4 of the book. The professional and personal support given me by Maryann Gialanella Valiulis and Anthony Valiulis, who know

the meaning of friendship, helped sustain me through the difficult times. Finally, I want to thank my husband, Chip Radding,
without whom, clichéd as it sounds, this book might never have
been written. His willingness to read my manuscript and to contribute his historical insights in the midst of writing his own
books improved this work immeasurably; his firm belief that
half the family-raising responsibility was his and that half the
computer time was mine made this book possible.

CHARTER REFORM IN CHICAGO

THE GENESIS OF AN URBAN VISION

When a group of Chicago residents began to campaign for a new municipal charter in 1902, they were part of a national charter reform movement and, in a broader sense, of the national progressive reform movement sweeping the country in the late nineteenth and early twentieth centuries. The municipal problems they perceived were common ones. Overlapping administrative and fiscal authorities operated within cities, blurring the lines of municipal responsibility; restrictions on taxing and bonding powers seriously limited the financial resources of cities and hampered their abilities to make improvements; and the franchise system gave cities little control over the supply and distribution of public services. These problems existed because state municipal laws had been written earlier in the century when there were few large cities in the United States. Thus, they addressed the needs of small towns and moderately sized cities more than those of large urban areas such as Chicago.[1] However, because cities in the United States are the legal creations of their state governments, reform of the laws under which they governed themselves could not be accomplished by the cities alone. They had to persuade state legislatures to enact new laws for their municipalities.

For Chicago, securing a new municipal charter was not going to be an easy task. The Illinois Constitution of 1870 did not charter individual cities. Rather, it provided a single general incorporation act that applied to all cities and towns in the state regardless of their size. Thus, a new charter applying only to Chicago was entirely outside the scope of the existing laws. Moreover, this incorporation act reserved significant powers to the state legislature. It carefully enumerated which particular powers a municipality could exercise and conferred no general or reserve powers on cities that might have given them latitude to respond to new needs and circumstances as they arose.[2] To overcome these obstacles meant convincing the state government to treat Chicago differently from the rest of the cities in the state and to relinquish some of the legislature's own prerogatives by granting home rule powers to Chicago alone.

Despite many potential obstacles to this undertaking, many Chicago residents believed that a new charter was an absolute necessity, and they gladly turned their attentions to securing such a document. Between 1902 and 1907, a group of citizens wrote a new charter which, with some difficulties and modifications, did pass through the state legislature. But the voters of the city rejected this charter. In 1909 and then again in 1914–15, more modified charter reforms were proposed, but these met with the same results. The effort to reform Chicago's municipal charter was subsequently abandoned. Chicago's new charter movement failed, and the city moved into the twentieth century with a municipal government inadequate to meet the needs of a modern industrial city.

Why did charter reform fail in Chicago when it succeeded in many cities across the country? This is the broad question of this book. To find the answer to this and other questions regarding Chicago's subsequent political development, it is essential first to understand that Chicago, like all cities, has its own political culture. Used historically, the term *political culture* differs in meaning from the same term used by political scientists.[3] In historical terms, it means that each city possesses a set of particular historical circumstances developed over time. These include the past experiences of citizens' dealings with each other on important political issues. And these experiences in turn help determine the outcome of future political and municipal decisions.

By the time Chicagoans considered charter reform, their previous political experiences influenced its course. At no point during the charter campaign could Chicago escape the ramifications of its political culture, particularly because, as the book will show, the clashes over these earlier issues had created a strong climate of political awareness among the citizenry. In Chicago, four circumstances had shaped the configurations of its political culture by the early twentieth century. The first circumstance was an antipathy between Chicago and the rest of the state, which grew increasingly severe through the second half of the nineteenth century. The second circumstance was the ongoing labor strife within the city itself; hostilities between business and labor were often as acute as those between the city and the state. The battle over temperance, always a controversial urban issue in late-nineteenth-century American cities, also played an important role in the development of Chicago's political culture. Finally, disagreements over who in the city spoke for reform, and what kind of reform, contributed to the making of Chicago's political culture.

The concept of a city's ongoing political culture, however, has not been applied to the study of urban reform movements in the Progressive Era. Indeed, work on the subject has revolved around altogether opposite concepts as a short review of the recent historiography shows. Underpinning much of the recent work on urban reform have been two theoretical premises about cities. The first premise assumes that individual cities are primarily parts of the organic whole—the nation—in which specifically local concerns are, at best, tertiary. When urban historians discarded the original urban biography approach of studying cities as too narrow in scope, they turned away from viewing the political history of individual cities as a whole. They sought instead to find ways to examine the complexities of urban reform as a national phenomenon expressed in local variants.[4] Thus, "case studies" of specific reform measures in different cities have proliferated, and, within them, there is little room for viewing the city as a whole. The very term "case study" implies that pieces can be studied as part of the whole, that they are indeed interchangeable. Once this assumption has been incorporated into any case study, the results are skewed toward this perspective.[5]

The second premise assumes that an interest-group construct is a viable one to apply to the study of urban political history. Political scientists use this construct to study political and governmental processes. For them, an interest group is "a shared-attitude group that makes certain claims upon other groups. . . . If and when it makes its claims through or upon any of the institutions of government, it becomes a political interest group."[6] The interest-group construct operates on the premise that different population elements can be isolated from each other and categorized according to economic or social interests that are easily recognized, fairly static, and easily measured. It also assumes that these categories themselves can tell us about political interests. To discover what reforms were undertaken during the Progressive Era and why, historians have attempted to utilize this construct by dividing city residents into interest groups. The city in the Progressive Era has been seen as composed of reformers or nonreformers, structural reformers or social reformers, old middle-class, new middle-class, upper-class, or even ethnic working-class reformers. Cities themselves have been divided into working-class spread cities or middle-class spread cities, ethnic cities or heavily Protestant cities.[7]

Among the problems raised by this approach is the fact that if some people were seen as reformers, others, by definition, had to be excluded from this category. And there had to be some significant differences between the two groups, that is, there had to be some reason why one group was reform and one group was not. The explanation most often proposed was that a "progressive" few among urban residents had developed a "cosmopolitan" vision of the city by the early twentieth century. This cosmopolitan vision enabled them to see the city as a whole and plan for reform accordingly. On the other hand, the views of the majority of a city's residents remained "local." Trapped in their localist perspective, they remained concerned only about what piece of the pie was going to be theirs and ignored the shape of the whole municipal pie. Thus, they did not support progressive reforms aimed at reshaping the whole city.

Justifiably, certain historians reacted against this pronouncement that the majority of urban residents were antireform and sought to show that this majority had its own legitimate concerns about urban reform measures. To do so, they proposed the dichotomy of ethnoculturism. According to the ethnoculturists, people in the Progressive Era fell into two opposing camps based on their ethnic religious orientation: they were either pietists or ritualists. Pietists were largely the Anglo-Saxon Protestant middle class. They favored urban reform proposals because their ethnocultural orientation led them to believe in right action. Ritualists were Catholic ethnic immigrants for the most part. They opposed these reforms because their emphasis on right belief led them to shun any reform measures that looked to them like government legislation of moral or social affairs. Ritualists sought "a government of severely restricted scope, a government whose presence could be seen but not felt. The ideological expression of their concept of good government was aptly enunciated in the 'personal liberty' slogan."[8]

The ethnocultural argument contains two fundamental problems. First of all, it rests its case largely on one issue—prohibition—arguing that ethnic opposition to prohibition stemmed from an aversion to government regulation of morality. That same reasoning is then seen behind the ritualists' rejection of other progressive reform proposals. But why develop a whole theoretical apparatus to explain why people who liked drinking in social situations and looked upon it as an integral part of their daily lives opposed prohibition? It is obvious why they opposed it. One might better ask, why should they support it?

But a more troubling problem is that while the purpose of the ritualist/pietist dichotomy was to liberate immigrant groups from the disparaging label of nonreformer, it disparages them in a different fashion. It portrays them as people steadfastly clinging to old traditions and supposed cultural norms, unwilling, if not unable, to respond to new cultural situations. It cannot credit urban immigrants with having their own vision of the city as a whole or with having different but equally valid ideas about the nature of good government.[9] The personal liberty slogan, as will be shown in subsequent chapters, was a slogan. It was a rhetorical device that expressed in one simple term a complex network of ideas about the role of government, the nature of urban life, the relationship between urban and rural populations, and the kind of city people wanted to result from urban reforms. In Chicago, for example, the very groups to whom the ethno-cultural interpretation has been applied supported municipal ownership. This reform would have greatly enhanced the scope of the municipal government's powers. It is hard to reconcile this stance with one that favors a "government severely restricted in scope."

Kathleen Neils Conzen has recently directed attention to the habit historians have developed of borrowing from sociology the idea that there is a link "between urban growth and consequent social and personal disorganization."[10] According to this idea, mass urbanization first created problems that could not be solved by "traditional means." Thus, *gemeinschaft* gave way to *gesellschaft*, the "public community" replaced the "private city," and public institutions, including government and social or professional organizations, assumed the functions once performed by individuals. These new impersonal groups acted as arbiters of social values and social norms for the city as a whole.[11]

When placed in a historical perspective, this formulation raises questions. Urbanization, for one thing, was certainly not a new phenomenon in the late nineteenth century. Where do seventeenth-century London, or fourteenth-century Venice, or first-century Rome fit into the equation? Each city placed in its own historical context would reveal a differing sense of urban community developed over time. Moreover, it is not at all clear that the historical evidence supports the theory. The community theory is a hypothesis and not a fact. Urban historians have seldom questioned its underlying theoretical assumptions about how society works. They have not always paid close attention to the historical data or probed too deeply to see if urban residents in the Progressive Era were actually talking about that kind of community or not.[12]

Part of the problem with adopting the community theory is that it tends to see all change as being forced by material circumstance. For the late nineteenth century and the Progressive Era, such circumstances as the "inherent impersonality of large-scale urban existence," wherein "city dwellers breathed the same sooty air, drank the same poisoned water, slogged the same muddy streets, shared the same crowded streetcars and the same fatal diseases" are interpreted as undermining "traditional community" and forcing a change in thinking about how to cope with urban problems.[13] In Chicago, for example, the new view of urban life held by one prominent citizen has been explained as a view that came not "through study and reflections . . . but that had been forged for him in the fire of 1871."[14]

But with the exception of the crowded streetcars, the above description of late-nineteenth-century cities could as easily be applied to the conditions of thirteenth-century Paris as to late-nineteenth-century New York City. And if circumstance alone forced change, why was not this view forged for someone out of the disastrous fire that burned London to the ground in 1666 or any number of urban catastrophes throughout Western history? Thus, it cannot be simply circumstance that was forcing urban residents to adopt the new attitudes toward their daily existence that appeared in the late nineteenth century.

Yet, if it was not circumstance that forced change, where did the impetus come from? The answer is that it was not the experience alone, but rather what people did with and thought of their urban experiences that began to produce ideas about reform. For the first time among residents of Western cities, there was developing a conscious vision of the city as a whole, of the effects which all parts had on the whole, and a desire to control and shape the whole urban environment.

In overlooking the interaction of circumstances and ideas, of experience with thought, the very active roles that urban residents played in reshaping their cities in the Progressive Era is obscured. The question of why people were thinking differently about circumstances that in many real aspects had existed in large cities for centuries is not asked. This is especially true when this approach divides residents into those who have developed a new cosmopolitan vision and those who are still stuck in the old "traditional" ways of thinking. If one group of people and their ideas are isolated from the rest of the people in the city, the rhetoric used by each side cannot be tested against the reality.

Ideas about cities as places to live have received minor consideration in the study of urban reform movements. Because historians in so many other fields have begun to question the role of *mentalité* in shaping societies, this omission is curious. *Mentalité* assumes the existence of, and seeks out, the continuing local character of historical development. Viewing progressive reform movements as manifestations of political culture can highlight this local character.

To analyze these movements in such a way requires a more dynamic reading of the processes of urban reform. It necessitates both trying to understand what participants intended as a result of their stance on reform issues and recognizing that ideas are not the passive products of a person's (or group's) place in society defined by interest-group or class needs. Rather, ideas are active instruments through which people assess and try to shape their society. When these ideas are articulated, they reveal what urban residents intended as the result of their stand on reform proposals. These intentions, in turn, show their conceptions of a desirable urban life. It has been suggested that the achievement of the groups heretofore identified as reformers was to replace "nineteenth century notions of laissez-faire and limited governmental functions with the concept of public responsibility for the welfare of all urban dwellers." [15] The unspoken assumption here is that no other urban residents had made a similar shift in their ideas about the city. As such, this analysis foregoes the possibility that there may have developed a contrary concept of public responsibility. If, instead of equating reform movements such as Chicago's new charter movement and its supporters with a "cosmopolitan" urban vision and those who opposed it with a "local" outlook, historians asked new questions of the wealth of material at hand, the dynamics of urban politics in this era could become clearer.

The sources available for studying Chicago's charter reform movement provide the possibilities for studying urban reform movements in this fashion. They are both abundant and revealing of the ideas circulating at the time about cities. First, they show Chicagoans thinking about the city as a whole, not just about their particular ethnic or geographic or class interests. They show in the arguments and actions over charter reform that Chicagoans knew they were taking a very important step toward restructuring their municipal government, but that they did not agree about what kind of urban environment they wanted to create for the city as a whole. The reform campaign provided for them a vehicle for arguing about and redefining a desirable urban existence. And their conflicting desires determined whether they supported or opposed specific reform proposals.

The materials on charter reform also reveal how, at every stage of the reform process, the city's political culture influenced that process. Fear of the state legislature, old wounds from labor strife, past battles over prohibition and over political reform in general—none of these, individually, determined the position assumed by Chicagoans on charter reform, but taken together as past history, they greatly illuminate the reasons for the charter's failure.

Third, these materials provide suggestions for understanding Chicago's subsequent political development. The failure of charter reform left the city tied to an outmoded form of municipal government. The overall campaign for reform was the breeding ground of political attitudes that would carry over into the succeeding decades. Chicago's municipal government was never structurally centralized. Because the old system could not continue to function indefinitely into the twentieth century, a fact acknowledged by citizens on both sides of the charter issue, Chicago had to find another path to change. That change was the political machine that emerged in the early 1930s and imposed de facto centralization on Chicago. Chicago, in the 1910s, thus had more in common with Chicago of the 1890s and 1930s than it did with New York in these periods, and neither metropolis greatly resembled Galveston or Rochester. Returning to the sources and paying closer attention to what people in Chicago said they wanted their city to be reveals clearly how the ideas of Progressive-Era urban reform developed within the context of the political culture of urban life itself.

ONE

CITY OF PROGRESS, CITY OF PROBLEMS

Political Culture and the Urban Context of Charter Reform

> But there is another side to Chicago. There is the back side to her fifteen hundred million dollars of trade, her seventeen thousand vessels, and her ninety thousand miles of rail.
> —George Steevens

Chicagoans entered the last decade of the nineteenth century proud of their city's achievements and brimming with enthusiasm for its future. Only a few of them were concerned that a number of nagging municipal problems had cropped up which showed no signs of going away, and certainly no one envisioned the political machine of the future. Even those citizens aware of the problems were certain that they could find the right solutions. Instead of dwelling on possible problems, they looked forward to 1893 as their opportunity to dazzle world visitors with the city's beauty and progress. That year, the Columbian Exposition opened on the south side of Chicago. The exposition's gleaming "White City" with its magnificent esplanade flanked by pavilions and exhibit halls evoked the past and future. The architecture was neoclassical; but inside were displays of the most modern achievements of the new industrial, technological society to which Chicago so proudly belonged. Both sides of the exposition drew appropriate expressions of awe from an array of international spectators. A traveler from India thought the

fair "a spectacle that exceeded all my expectations of gran-
deur." "This ethereal emanation of pure and uneconomic beauty"
startled a Scottish writer. French diplomat Francois Bruwaert
surely warmed the hearts of the city fathers when he equated
the fair with the city itself, predicting that "the most beautiful
exhibition will be Chicago itself, its citizens, its business, its institutions, its progress." The city's vibrance, "the sight of so many
ways open to human industry; the sight of so many natural resources," attracted the Italian playwright Giuseppe Giacosce.[1]

No one could deny Chicago its economic and technological
achievements over the twenty years preceding the Columbian
Exposition. The city had emerged from the fire of 1871 badly
scarred but determined to rebuild its institutions. The nation-
wide depression of 1873 slowed but could not blunt the city's re-
growth. It was fortunate for Chicago's economic recovery that
the Union Stockyards and over three-fourths of the city's grain
elevators and lumberyards had escaped the fire. Burned-out
plants and factories in other areas of the city, including the
McCormick Reaper Works, were quickly rebuilt. Within a few
years, Chicago's economic prominence in meatpacking, live-
stock, grain, and lumber had been restored. The fire had also
spared the railroad freight terminals on the edge of the city, and
to these the railroad companies soon added new passenger terminals within the city, leaving goods and people once again to
flow easily and quickly through the city.

The force of external events combined with the vigor of the
city's residents to expand and alter the economy in the succeeding years. Between 1870 and 1890, as millions of people moved
into the midwest, the population center of the United States
advanced westward over one hundred miles, leaving eastern
manufacturing and industrial cities inaccessible to these people.
Chicago, with its great transportation network and thriving
business community, became the obvious locale for shipping raw
materials to be finished and distributed to customers for both
commercial and industrial purposes. In no time, the industrial-
ization of Chicago was well underway. Heavy industry, including
the Illinois Steel Company, the Pullman Palace Car Company,
the Grant Locomotive Works, and several new firms building

trolley cars, found congenial homes in the city. Six of the city's factories, including the McCormick Reaper Works (later International Harvester), produced one-seventh of the country's agricultural implements. Light industry and manufacturing also prospered: the printing and publishing industries in Chicago were soon second only to those in New York; clothing and dry goods manufacturing and selling and the ready-to-wear women's and children's garment business joined the already thriving men's wear establishments to form the only clothing center in the country to rival New York's garment district. New mercantile houses and retail stores kept Chicago a commercial center as well. The country's two largest catalog stores—Montgomery Ward, the first national mail-order company, which began operations in 1872, and Sears, Roebuck and Company—and several major department stores, including Marshall Field and Company, were headquartered in Chicago. By the end of the nineteenth century, Chicago was unquestionably the premier city of the midwest.[2]

Side by side with its economic advancement, Chicago, in the twenty-five years after the fire, was determined not to be outdone by any other city in its implementation of the kinds of technological innovations that were steadily altering and reshaping the appearance of late-nineteenth-century cities. Trolley tracks and Elevated structures changed the contours of the city streets to provide enormous new opportunities for movement through the city. Above and beneath those streets, electric power cables, telephone lines, gas pipes, water pipes, and sewer systems carried the newest technological advances into homes and businesses.

The rapid expansion of Chicago's public transit system exemplified how quickly these changes proceeded. By the end of the century, streetcar tracks crisscrossed the city. Eighty-six miles of cable car track had been laid by 1894, but by the time the cable cars began to function, they were already obsolete, surpassed by the new technology of the electric trolleys that were being run experimentally along the old horse-drawn trolley tracks. Because the electric trolley proved far less costly to operate than the cable cars and traveled at double the speed of the horse-drawn ones, the horses were quickly relegated to pasture and the cable cars to the museum. Soon electric trolleys were running along more than five hundred miles of track, leaving the city prey to the horrendous traffic jams that can be seen in turn-of-the-century photographs of Chicago.

Even as the street tracks were being laid, yet another form of mass transit arrived in Chicago. With an eye on alleviating traffic congestion, the South Side Rapid Transit Company began constructing an elevated line on the south side in 1890. Using steam locomotives and freed from the constraints of traffic, the el carried passengers at the previously unheard-of rate of fifteen miles an hour. Within three years, a west side el moved overhead along Lake Street. By the end of the decade, the Northwestern Elevated Railroad reached to Wilson Avenue, a street that just eleven years earlier had been almost three miles north of the city limits. By 1906, Chicago possessed more than eighty miles of elevated track that took commuters on an eye-level ride along the first-floor windows of office buildings and homes. Simultaneously, the city had doubled the total of its street railway surface.[3]

These economic and technological advancements were accompanied by a massive population growth that helped make Chicago a city of major proportions by the end of the century. People streamed into the city to fill the rapidly multiplying number of jobs. One half million people lived in Chicago in 1880. Ten years later, the population had doubled. By 1900, it stood at almost 1.7 million. The annexation by the city of surrounding townships accounted for part of this growth: between 1880 and 1890, for example, the population of "old" Chicago rose from 503,000 to 792,000, with the remaining increase coming from annexed townships. Still, prior to annnexation, these surrounding townships themselves were growing rapidly, and whether people were migrating directly into the city or to its suburbs, they were in fact coming to Chicago. Until 1889, for instance, the Union Stockyards were located outside the city limits; thus, many of the immigrants who found jobs in the stockyards and housing near their work actually lived outside the city proper.

Besides, it was not long before the townships became consolidated into the city. The pressures of a wildly expanding population combined with the promises of cheaper land and the availability of mass transit to draw large numbers of people and industry into the townships around the city during the 1870s and 1880s. The population of Hyde Park township to the south increased almost ninefold from 15,700 to 133,000 during the 1880s; that of Lake township to the west went from 18,000 to just over 100,000 in the same decade.[4] The mass of people moving into the townships and the public transit lines leapfrogged each other in the rush out of the city. Transit lines sometimes preceded people. At other times, new areas of settlement created the demand for the extension of transportation services. As a result, the commuter railroads, by the late 1880s, carried twenty-seven-thousand daily commuters into the city, with cable cars and the new electric street railways transporting thousands more. Streetcar lines along Evanston (now Broadway), Clark, Lincoln, and Milwaukee avenues and expanded service on the Chicago and Northwestern and the Chicago, Milwaukee and St. Paul railroads served people in the north townships of Lake View, Rogers Park, and Edgewater, and northwest Jefferson Park. On the other side of the city, the Rock Island line ran to the southwest townships of Beverly and Morgan Park, while the Illinois Central and the streetcar lines along Cottage Grove Avenue connected Hyde Park to the city proper. Only to the west did Chicago's expansion proceed more slowly, perhaps deterred by a reluctance to leave the city's best physical asset, its beautiful lake front, and by the presence of large immigrant slums immediately west of the central city.

The flood of people into the townships, however, very quickly overburdened their small governments. It was not long before groups of people in the townships, as well as in the city, began to consider the possible benefits of annexation to Chicago. For some township dwellers, annexation seemed the most sensible way to relieve the seemingly insurmountable fiscal problems that had appeared almost simultaneously with settlement. Under the existing system, each township had to finance its own public utilities, school system, police and fire departments, and other essential services. Providing such public services became increasingly difficult as the population expanded because many of these townships were commuter suburbs with little industry. Hence, they lacked the necessary tax base to subsidize these services. Even residents of those areas with a broader tax base promoted annnexation, believing either that their local police forces were too small and weak to control growing labor problems or hoping that it would rid them of existing political corruption. Almost all the townships coveted the city's well-developed water-supply system. For their part, many Chicagoans favored annexation as a way to recapture the wealth and industry that had fled to the townships and to acquire the people and territory to make Chicago into a great metropolitan area.

With sentiment favoring annexation thus growing in both the city and townships, the Citizens' Association of Chicago began to campaign actively for its implementation. In 1887, the group asked the General Assembly of Illinois to enact a law permitting willing townships to consolidate their governments with the city. When the legislature agreed, citizens from Hyde Park, Lake, Lake View, Cicero, and Jefferson Park townships petitioned for annexation. The desire to consolidate with the city was not unanimous among suburbanites, of course. Some of them predicted that dire consequences would result from joining with the city. They pointed out that many township dwellers had fled the city to escape its growing municipal problems, and that annexation would invite those problems into the smaller areas.

The matter was put before township voters in a special referendum in November of the same year. Without overwhelming support for annexation, the result of this referendum was mixed. The citizens of Lake and Lake View rejected annexation; those in Hyde Park, Cicero, and Jefferson Park voted to join the city. But the entire referendum was negated several months later when the Illinois Supreme Court ruled the annexation law unconstitutional. Disappointed, but not daunted, the annexationists reorganized their campaign. Two years later, they secured a new state law and prepared another referendum. The Chicago City Council helped the cause this time by passing two ordinances designed to overcome the fears of some of the suburbanites still opposing annexation. These ordinances guaranteed the preservation of existing township prohibition districts after incorporation and prohibited the extension of Chicago building codes, meager as they were, to new areas without their consent.

This time, the annexation forces were completely successful, despite the opposition of some powerful businessmen. George Pullman, for instance, had vigorously resisted the incorporation of his company town; and meatpacker Philip Armour had made a deal with the local politicians of Lake township to oppose annexation in return for a new low tax assessment on his company property. But the once reluctant voters of Hyde Park, Lake, Lake View, Cicero, and Jefferson Park now voted to become part of Chicago.

The city continued to annex suburban areas for the next four years. In 1893, the far north townships of Rogers Park and West Ridge joined Chicago; a few small areas on the western periphery were added later, but Chicago's geographic expansion essentially ended at this point. All totaled, the city's area had increased from thirty-five to one hundred and ninety square miles, making Chicago indeed a great metropolitan area by the year of the Columbian Exposition.[5]

The Pitfalls of Progress

With the completion of the annexation movement, Chicago ended the nineteenth century no longer a fairly compact commercial city strung out along the shore of Lake Michigan. It had grown into a geographical, industrial, and demographical giant with municipal problems to match its size. Such rapid development had strained the city's physical and financial resources to their limits, producing a seamy side to the city that many of its visitors in 1893 and thereafter did not miss. Even as the British journalist George Steevens duly noted the city's economic progress, he simultaneously wrote about the back side of the city where "away from the towering offices, lying off from the smiling parks, is a vast wilderness of shabby houses." And Giuseppe Giacosce, for all his appreciation of the city's beauty, was appalled by its general condition. "I would not want to live there for anything in the world. . . . I did not see anything in Chicago but darkness: smoke, clouds, dirt and an extraordinary number of sad and grieved persons." Another famous British visitor, Rudyard Kipling, considered Chicago a vulgar and unlivable place. "Having seen it," he declared, "I urgently desire never to see it again. It is inhabited by savages." Taking the Palmer House, one of the city's most elegant hotels, as a metaphor for the city as a whole, Kipling saw "a gilded and mirrored rabbit-warren . . . a huge hall of tessellated marble, crammed with people talking about money and spitting about everywhere."[6]

Even granting that Kipling thought everything about the United States vulgar and uncivilized, there was no denying that Chicago had another, dirtier side from that displayed in the exposition. It could not be denied that industrial advancement and population growth had produced enormous municipal problems that the city was not handling well. As was the case with all the expanding cities across the country, Chicago faced a housing crisis. All the newcomers that came to stoke the city's industrial machine needed places to live. But by the end of the century, Chicago's housing stock was inadequate and already badly deteriorated.

Unlike residents of older, more crowded eastern cities, Chicagoans before the fire had lived in single-family dwellings that inefficiently used the city's limited available land. After 1871, multi-family flats had been constructed especially along streetcar routes to try to redress this impractical land usage pattern. By the end of the decade, the six-flat had become a popular form of housing. While many such apartment buildings were well-constructed and pleasant places to live, larger wooden, cheaply built tenements also appeared and these often were not conducive to good living conditions. The chief virtue of these large tenements, of course, was that they housed many families within a small area. However, the practice of housing as many people in as small an area as possible lent itself easily to abuse. Builders crammed together as many tenements as possible, leaving little or no passageway between buildings, sometimes erecting new tenements in front of existing buildings situated on the back of a lot, and often joining these buildings into one large structure—the so-called double-decker. In the older parts of the city, even the existing small, frame single-family houses were subdivided to accommodate several families. "Street stretches beyond street of little houses, mostly wooden, begrimed with soot, rotting, falling to pieces" was how George Steevens described these areas as he walked through the poorer sections of the city.[7]

But cheap housing was needed, so the crowded tenements proliferated. The Department of Health officially assessed the state of much of the tenement housing in 1896 as "old, dilapidated or rotten, unventilated, badly lighted, badly drained, unprovided with proper facilities for disposal of excreta and without adequate or even necessary water supply." Five years later, a private survey of three Chicago neighborhoods confirmed the department's earlier findings. Although the city's health commissioners had asked the city council since 1872 to regulate conditions within and around tenements, the incessant need for cheap housing and a reluctance to interfere with private property continually frustrated these requests. Chicago entered the new century with no comprehensive building and sanitary code, and the few building codes actually enacted were freely violated.[8]

Appalling exterior conditions in many parts of the city often accompanied the poor housing stock. Garbage piled up rapidly in the streets and alleys, sewer systems were hopelessly outdated in many parts of the city, the streets themselves were often unpaved, unrepaired, and seldom cleaned. The private firms hired to collect garbage seldom fulfilled their contracts in tenement neighborhoods, and the ward garbage inspectors were political appointees who, likewise, tended to ignore their responsibilities. Landlords contributed to the problems by providing too few collection boxes for their buildings, allowing garbage to overflow and litter the streets, alleys, and yards.[9]

The city had tried to redress some of these problems at the time of the Columbian Exposition, resurfacing over one thousand miles of streets and doubling the number of city sidewalks between 1889 and 1893. But only certain areas of the city benefited from these improvements, and just three years after the fair closed, another visitor to Chicago found the sidewalks "nothing but rotten planks in the slum streets, with great holes rendering it positively dangerous to walk in the dark."[10]

The changing character of Chicago's population by the end

of the century also contributed to creating serious social and economic problems in the city. For the most part, the new residents were foreign-born. They and their children composed roughly seventy-five percent of the total population for the two decades from 1890 to 1910, giving Chicago a greater percentage of foreign stock residents than any other major American city except New York and Milwaukee. Chicago also had the highest percentage of foreign-born residents outside of New York and Boston.[11] Industrial growth had not yet attracted large numbers of black migrants from the south. Although their aggregate numbers increased ten times between 1870 and 1900, black Chicagoans remained only 1.9 percent of the total populace at the turn of the century, so they cannot be said to have altered the population balance much at all. Rather, it was the new immigrants who concerned Chicagoans.

In the previous decades the nature of immigration into the city had been different. Then, the numbers of immigrants had been smaller, some of them at least spoke English, and a certain percentage of them were educated or skilled craftsmen. For a while the city had been able to absorb many of these immigrants into its existing structures. First- and second-generation Germans, Scandinavians, and even Irish could be found in most professions and businesses in the city before the turn of the century. However, the nationalities of the immigrants moving into the city changed decisively by the beginning of the twentieth century. Eastern and southern Europeans replaced the earlier arrivees. This trend alarmed the older residents for several reasons, not the least of course being that the newcomers looked different and rarely spoke English, but also because the overwhelming majority came from entirely different social and economic backgrounds. They were poor, largely uneducated, and unskilled, coming into an industrial city from a rural background. Added to these difficulties was the fact that they were coming in such vast numbers.

Chicago could not absorb the newcomers gracefully. It was impossible to provide enough cheap housing for them. The public school system did not have the resources to cope with an influx of new pupils, most of whom did not speak English. It could neither afford to pay for the new facilities that were necessary to accomodate these children, nor pay the many more teachers that were needed to staff the system. During the depression years of the late nineteenth century, the city had neither the financial nor legal means to help this great pool of unskilled industrial laborers and their families.

Adding to the city's difficulties in providing adequate housing and external sanitation, clean and well maintained streets and sidewalks, and enough employment and educational opportunities, were the problems caused by the franchise system by which most public utilities were run. In the nineteenth century, franchising was the common way of providing such municipal services as public transit, gas, electricity, and telephones. Under this system, the municipal government granted private businesses the rights to build and make the profits from utilities in return for some monetary concessions to the city. One of the shortcomings of the franchise system was that it offered the chance of enormous profits to greedy entrepreneurs and corrupt city officials. All across the country, these men milked the system for personal gain regardless of the consequences for the city.[12]

Unfortunately for the people of Chicago, their city council was among the most corrupt. Led by Johnny Powers and his "grey wolves," the honorable aldermen had perfected the art of franchise graft and their skills had earned the council a national reputation. The "grey wolves" sold street franchises for all public utilities one block at a time to the highest bidders. This practice drove up utility costs because the successful bidders simply passed their expenses along to the customers; it also resulted in multiple systems along one street. Perhaps the most notable franchise coup of the council came in the gas trust scandals of the 1890s. In 1894, the aldermen passed the universal gas ordinance which, after receipt of a suitable fee, gave the Gas Trust (nine companies combined specifically for this purpose) the rights to lay gas mains anywhere in the city. A year later, several aldermen pushed through the council a measure granting another group, the Ogden Gas Trust, a fifty-year franchise in the city that included blanket rights to the city streets as long as it sold gas at ninety cents per 1000 cubic feet. Because the original

Gas Trust sold its gas at $1.20, this new franchise was presumably going to cut the former out of the market. The catch was that Ogden Gas existed only on paper. The ordinance was a blatant attempt to force the Gas Trust to buy up the rights of Ogden Gas, which of course it did, the money going straight into the aldermen's pockets.[13]

The aldermen could manipulate the franchise system so freely because whatever municipal powers Chicago possessed rested with the council. Under this strong-council form of municipal government, the aldermen drew up the municipal budget, created new boards and departments within the existing government, accepted and rejected all mayoral appointments, enacted a broad range of municipal ordinances, and controlled the distribution of city jobs and franchises. In the hands of less than scrupulous people, late-nineteenth-century Chicago politics was often a free-for-all affair. Jobs, franchises, and favorable ordinances were for sale; and any faction holding a majority of seats could, and often did, thwart the desires of both the mayor and the rest of the council members.[14]

The circumstances of urban, industrial, technological growth thus had placed Chicago's municipal government in a precarious position by the late nineteenth century. But it was not simply the force of circumstances that began to move Chicagoans in the Progressive Era toward looking for new solutions to their urban problems and for new ways in which to control their environment. It was rather the coincidence of these circumstances with the growing awareness of them as communal problems and as problems that quite conceivably could be solved.

Technological innovations had certainly created an entirely new kind of urban environment. Mass transit, telephones, electricity, and other services brought the conveniences of modern life to urban residents. But they also inevitably linked homes and apartment buildings, stores and businesses, factories and shops, private enterprise and public concerns into a much more closely knit urban fabric than ever before. This was a result that could not adequately, if at all, have been seen beforehand. Not only did individuals clamor for the technology for themselves, they wanted it spread throughout the city to enhance business

and daily life in general. Such technological expansion, however, was highly expensive, and very quickly cities faced the continuing crisis of how to fund such technology.

Furthermore, as technological advancements spread, the
bulk of urban residents became much more dependent on the
continued building and maintenance of the services. For example, once both employers and employees began to count on
public transportation to bring people to their jobs, an urban crisis of major proportions could ensue if the systems deteriorated,
were struck, or went bankrupt. Unlike seventeenth-century
Paris, where a small horse-drawn omnibus system failed and
quietly disappeared after a few years despite its popularity,[15]
Chicago, as it arrived at the twentieth century, could not afford
to let such a thing happen. Technology had created a different
kind of urban network and this network depended on mass transit, as well as on the continued service of telephones, gas, electricity, and water.[16] For these services to work well required a
higher degree of organization than had existed in cities up to the
end of the century, as the failures of the franchise system were
proving all too well.

At the same time, attitudes toward nontechnological matters had begun to change within Chicago. Many of the city's residents were coming to believe that all those newcomers needed
decent places to live and their children needed schools; that the
streets ought to be paved and cleaned; that garbage should be
more efficiently and effectively removed and sanitation conditions be improved throughout the city; and that police and fire
protection needed to be upgraded. The urban conditions themselves had not changed so greatly from those that had prevailed
in large cities for centuries. The streets of late-nineteenth-
century Chicago were certainly no worse than those of Boston or
New York a century earlier or of London a century before that.
For centuries, cities had been places where millions of urban
poor had lived in hovels far worse than those of Chicago's slums,
where rich and poor alike had died in massive fires that swept
through cities with no organized means for fighting them, and
where the vast majority of children never attended school. The
unique element in Chicago and other American cities in the late

nineteenth century was that urban residents had begun to think differently about the conditions themselves and that they had come to think about the welfare of the city as a whole. An increasingly industrial and technological culture had placed before their eyes the possibilities of solving urban problems. Within this context, the residents of cities had begun to develop new ideas about urban life and to think in specific terms of urban reform and how to accomplish it.

The Unwieldy Municipal Government

The first major obstacle Chicagoans faced in implementing urban reform was their old-style municipal government, which did not have the legal means to cope with the exigencies of urban change. One of the ways around this problem was to seek a municipal charter from the Illinois state government. In general, securing charter reform was a difficult undertaking because American cities are the legal creations of state governments that are often unwilling to surrender any of their prerogatives to cities. Illinois, as mentioned earlier, had a very restricted general incorporation act that applied to all cities and towns in the state, and Chicago faced the formidable task of convincing the legislature to abandon this general law for legislation pertaining only to Chicago.

Many Chicago residents were willing to make the effort because they believed that a new charter would be an absolute necessity by the turn of the century. To keep within the existing state laws, Chicago's municipal government had evolved into a tortuous and cumbersome maze of overlapping administrative and fiscal authorities. Within the municipal boundaries, the Municipal Corporation, the Cook County Board of Commissioners, the Chicago Board of Education, the Chicago Library Board, three park boards, and the Metropolitan Sanitary District all operated as independent bodies, all distinct from each other in governing and taxing powers.

This situation had developed as a direct consequence of the limitations imposed upon the city by the state incorporation act. The sanitary district, for instance, had been created in 1889 because state law limited municipal indebtedness to one percent of the area's full property valuation. By the 1880s, Chicago had reached that figure and could not raise enough new revenue to construct desperately needed sewers and a drainage canal. The legislature would not change the tax laws, so the city could find recourse only in the formation of the Metropolitan Sanitary District. Ninety-two percent of the territory and 96 percent of the population serviced by this new body were within the city limits, but Chicago itself had no control over its activities. Instead, a nine-member board of trustees chose the district's minor officials, constructed all sewers, bought and sold real estate, borrowed money, issued bonds, and levied and collected taxes and special assessments.

Nor did Chicago exercise more control over other municipal services. The mayor selected the school-board and library-board members, but the powers of each board were delegated directly by the legislature. Each board also prepared its own budget and levied taxes independently of the city. The three park boards, created by the legislature in 1869, managed all park lands and levied taxes for park purposes within their individual jurisdictions. The County Board of Commissioners administered both the jail and the public hospital, even though these institutions were located in, and much more likely to be used by, the city because only 10 percent of the county's area and population was outside city limits. Duplication of vital public services abounded under this system. The city, the sanitary district, and each park board maintained separate police forces. The park boards operated their own electric light plants, and the Lincoln Park Board even had its own waterworks. These same boards paved, repaired, and cleaned the streets within individual properties, while the municipality provided this service to the remainder of the city. Besides being inefficient, this jerry-built structure created a wide disparity in how, and at what cost, these services were distributed among the city's residents. It was generally acknowledged, for instance, that the residents of the South Park district received far better services than those living within the other two districts.

Perhaps worst of all, from the point of view of many Chicagoans, was the city's disjointed revenue system, especially its fiscal relationship to the county government.[17] This body assessed Chicago's property, collected the taxes on it, and then remitted the monies back to the city on a schedule set by the state legislature. But there were other problems with the revenue system beyond the subservience to the county government. First, state law limited any one tax district to levying only a fixed percentage amount of property taxes from its assessed property values. Chicago was not its own tax district; rather, it was part of the Cook County district. Until 1901, this percentage, the tax base for Cook County, was not firmly fixed by law but had generally floated around 5 percent of all the county's assessed valuation. In that year, however, the Juul Law set the tax base at 5 percent.[18] Secondly, the Revenue Act of 1879 set Chicago's share of revenue for corporate purposes at 2 percent of this assessed property valuation and fixed the share of revenue going to the other governing authorities out of the remaining 3 percent of the allotted 5 percent tax base. Only the school board levies for school buildings and a portion of the sanitary district's taxes were exempt from these restrictions. This system assured that all governing bodies received a share of the tax revenues, but it was completely inflexible in the face of growing municipal problems. The city could not transfer funds from one taxing body with less need to another critically short of money. Nor was the city free to decide every year which areas were most in need and allocate the revenues accordingly. Mass immigration into the city had sorely overloaded the public school system, for instance, but the municipal government had no means for funneling more money in its direction.

Because property taxes were the major source of municipal revenues, the Juul Law and the Revenue Act had placed Chicago in a financially precarious position. By the end of the century, the city was continually strapped for revenue. Although cities in Illinois could also issue bonds to finance municipal projects, the state laws that limited the bonded indebtedness of any municipality to no more than 1 percent of its full property valuation greatly hindered Chicago also. Thus, when Chicago had reached this maximum in the 1880s, the result had been the creation of yet another independent district. Thereafter, the city often simply had to postpone undertaking improvements in municipal services because it had no money and no means for raising additional revenues. Streets, sidewalks, and sewers remained quite inadequate for the city's needs, but the Department of Public Works could do little to upgrade them for lack of funds.

These restrictions imposed by the state incorporation and revenue acts conspicuously hindered the city's ability to cope with growing urban problems. In addition to this problem, the traditional practice in the nineteenth century of franchising public utilities had left many services almost completely outside the city's jurisdiction. The problems this situation created were enormous. First, the city had virtually no control over the provision of these services once it granted the franchise. Thus, in Chicago, when the infamous traction magnate Charles Yerkes refused to run more cars on heavily traveled routes, declaring contemptuously that it was "the straphangers who pay the dividends,"[19] the city could not compel him to provide more streetcars. Second, the franchise system left Chicagoans at the mercy of the state legislators because they set the terms for granting municipal franchises. Third, the potential profits to be made from the system had produced mass bribery and corruption among entrepreneurs, city-council members, and state legislators. Yerkes, for example, had bought franchises block by block under different franchises and built more than one line along a route. He then refused to issue transfers between his routes and forced passengers to pay multiple fares. When Yerkes could not get what he wanted from the city council, he turned to his friends in the state legislature to pass new franchise laws, which they were too often willing to attempt in complete disregard of the needs of the people or the city as a whole.[20]

Given the magnitude of Chicago's municipal problems and the legal and structural inability of the municipal government to cope with them, the desire for a new charter was reasonable. A new charter could confer some home-rule powers on Chicago by relaxing the legal strictures that bound the city to the mercy of the state legislature. Simultaneously, it could alter the governing and taxing structures of the municipal government. Both changes promised relief for the city's increasingly complex and currently unmanageable municipal problems. And by the early twentieth century, the timing seemed right because many state legislators were willing to consider charter reform for Chicago. The legislators had tired of the constant flood of petitions from the city for special legislation, which was technically against the law, and the requests for constitutional amendments that kept coming from Chicago representatives.

Chicago's Political Culture

What then went wrong that Chicago never managed charter reform? The reasons for the failure of Chicago's charter reform movement were rooted in the dynamics of the city's political culture. To understand this political culture and its links to charter reform it is necessary to examine briefly the development of political life in Chicago prior to the proposed charter reform.

Four factors had been particularly important in shaping Chicago's political culture prior to the Progressive Era. The first factor was the long-standing antipathy between Chicago and the rest of the state. One of the continuing clues to understanding the mental conception that Chicagoans have always had of their relationship with the state is that, to this day, they still refer to most places outside of Cook County as "downstate," even when it is north or west of the city. In part, this historical antipathy stemmed from the differences in early settlement patterns in Illinois. Prior to the Civil War, settlers from the south and southeast followed the Ohio, Wabash, and Mississippi Rivers into southern and south-central Illinois. Migrants came into northern Illinois, on the other hand, from the northeast and mid-Atlantic areas via the Great Lakes and overland roads. Until the Illinois Central Railroad connected the state from north to south in 1856 the two areas of the state had relatively little contact with one another.[21] Sectional differences were then exacerbated by the sympathy rife in some southern parts of the state, the so-called "copperhead" areas, for the Confederate side during the war.

These broader north-south antagonisms had begun to narrow into a Chicago-downstate pattern of conflict by the time of Chicago's economic and population expansion after the 1871 fire. From 1871 onward, the city differed significantly from the rest of the state. In 1900, it was the only city of its size, popu-

lation mix, and industrial base in the state.[22] Demographic
changes in the last three decades of the nineteenth century
worsened the city-state antagonism because they threatened to
alter the balance of political power in the state. Each new federal census confirmed downstate fears that Chicago's population
would continue to grow while that of the rest of the state declined. Sixty-six percent of all rural areas and forty-nine counties in Illinois lost population between 1880 and 1900, while
Chicago's population tripled. Moreover, the city's foreign-born
population was double that of the rest of the state.[23]

From 1870 onward, downstate legislators, uncomfortably
aware of these alarming trends, sought to minimize the city's influence in the state legislature by trying to restrict permanently
the number of representatives from Chicago. They began their
campaign early, at the constitutional convention in 1870. Here
they attempted to have the new constitution replace proportional representation with representation by county, giving each
county an equal number of legislators regardless of size. Yet, in
1870, Chicago held only seven of the eighty-five seats in the legislature.[24] Their maneuver failed, but thereafter downstate representatives conducted a relentless campaign against Chicago.
Time and again they attempted to force the city to acquiesce in
permanent restriction or to accept general state laws opposed by
Chicagoans in exchange for legislation desired by the city. When
Chicago legislators refused to cooperate, their bills often died in
the legislature. At other times, the assembly enacted laws for
Chicago over the objections of its representatives.

Following the federal census of 1890, the situation worsened
for Chicago. In 1891, the legislature balked at reapportioning
the number of seats in the assembly. Nine reapportionment bills
were introduced before one finally passed in 1893. According to
the reapportionment in that year, the number of Chicago-Cook
County representatives increased by 50 percent to just under
one-third the total number of seats. A decade later, downstate
legislators again stalled reapportionment while they tried to
place a permanent restriction on Cook County's representation.
When finally forced to carry through the redistricting, they
found themselves faced with the situation they had feared for
years: Chicago emerged with one-third the membership of both

houses, enough votes to veto the bulk of state legislation that required a two-thirds majority.[25] In 1911, the legislature resolved the situation by simply refusing to reapportion because Chicago's representation would then have greatly exceeded one-third of the total legislators. Within such an acrimonious situation, any involvement of the state in Chicago's municipal affairs aroused immediate suspicion within the city. Because of the legal stature of the city, any attempt at charter reform was guaranteed to inflame these passions.

Labor strife within in Chicago formed the second factor in shaping Chicago's political culture. As an important industrial center, Chicago could not escape the increasingly radical labor activities that had spread to industrial areas throughout the country after the strike of 1877. The militant faction of labor organization caught fire in Chicago in 1884 when Albert Parsons founded the Central Labor Union. An anarchist who spurned the eight-hour movement in favor of abolishing the wage system altogether, Parsons attracted dissatisfied workers away from the more moderate Chicago Trades and Labor Assembly. Tensions within the city mounted quickly, fueled by hysterical stories in the major newspapers which, as one recent historian of Chicago's labor situation noted, "never failed to give the wildest utterances of the anarchists conspicuous display."[26] Lucy Parsons, one story warned, was urging "every dirty, lousy tramp [to] arm himself with a revolver or knife and lay in wait on the steps of the palaces of the rich."[27] Another apocryphal story charged "there are two dangerous ruffians at large in this city; two sneaking cowards who are trying to create trouble. . . . mark them for today. Keep them in view. Hold them personally responsible for any trouble that occurs."[28]

Businessmen responded with their own militance. After listening to the entreaties of Marshall Field, the Commercial Club gave the federal government land for Fort Sheridan. The members of the Merchants' Club donated land for building the Great Lakes Naval Training Station to ensure the presence of federal troops near Chicago.[29]

This growing militance quickly developed into armed violence. In the summer of 1885, the police, led by Inspector John "Black Jack" Bonfield, attacked striking streetcar workers undeterred by Mayor Carter Harrison's support for the strikers. The Chicago *Tribune* urged that violence be used to quash the strike by union sailors on the Great Lakes.[30] By early 1886, it was common for Chicagoans to witness "patrol-wagons filled with armed policemen dashing through the city."[31] Even when nonviolent, the demonstrations staged that spring by the labor movement frightened many Chicagoans. On April 25 the Central Labor Union held a massive demonstration along the lake front in support of the eight-hour workday. As many as 25,000 people took part in this demonstration. Barely a week later, Albert and Lucy Parsons and their two children led 80,000 workers in a May Day parade up Michigan Avenue. While the workers marched and sang, police, Pinkerton detectives, and deputized civilians crouched with rifles on the rooftops lining the parade route and the militia stood ready with their Gatling guns at the city's armories.[32]

It was in this heated atmosphere that the the Haymarket "massacre" of 1886 occurred. The background to the event was a strike at the McCormick Reaper Works, one of Chicago's oldest enterprises. In 1885, labor had forced the company to grant a 15 percent wage increase; now, a year later, McCormick provoked a strike by locking out unionized workers in an attempt to break the union. The company hired nonunion replacements and brought in the police and Pinkertons to protect them. Tension between the two sides turned to bloody confrontation when, on May 3, police fired into a crowd harassing the "scabs." Two union men were killed and several others wounded. The city's radical labor leaders summoned all laboring people to a protest meeting the next evening at Haymarket Square on the western edge of the central business district. Although tensions in the city remained high all the next day, and crowds clashed again with police at the reaper works, the gathering that evening was relatively small and the speeches were not very inflammatory. The scene stayed peaceful until the police, led by "Black Jack" Bonfield and acting against Mayor Carter Harrison's orders, waded into the crowd, ordering it to disperse. Then a bomb exploded in their midst, killing seven of the policemen.[33]

The reaction of the city leaders and businessmen was swift and unjust. Warning that a workers' revolution was imminent, newspapers, prominent citizens, and law enforcement officials hysterically accused the meeting's organizers of inciting violence and demanded that they be brought to trial for murder. Businessmen called for increased police vigilance against potential labor agitation and began forming their own citizens' vigilance groups; several of them formed themselves into the First Council of Conservators' League of America specifically to counteract these "recent labor troubles." At the same time, such luminaries of Chicago's business community as Cyrus McCormick (of the reaper works), Philip Armour, Marshall Field, and George Pullman helped form a Citizens' Association committee that volunteered its services to the police in these matters.[34]

Law enforcement officials were not any less vigilanteminded. State's attorney Julius S. Grinnell advised the police to "make the raids and look up the law afterward." The police responded with a ruthless sweep through working-class neighborhoods, rounding up trade unionists, foreigners, and just about anyone they wanted.[35] Eight men, including Albert Parsons, were accused, tried, and convicted in the press. "Public justice demands that the European assassins . . . shall be held, tried, and hanged for murder. Public justice demands that the assassin A. R. Parsons . . . shall be seized, tried, and hanged for murder," screamed a Chicago *Times* editorial. Nor did Parsons' wife Lucy escape the paper's invective: "Public justice demands that the negro woman who passes as the wife of the assassin Parsons . . . shall be seized, tried, and hanged for murder."[36] Lucy Parsons was not charged, but the eight men were convicted of murder before a judge and jury who were presented with no bomb thrower and no evidence linking the accused to the act. Despite some citizen protests against the injustice of the trial, in late 1887 four of these men were hanged. Governor John Altgeld subsequently pardoned the remaining three; the eighth man committed suicide in prison awaiting execution.

Haymarket strangled the radical labor movement in Chicago but the animosities it had engendered lingered.[37] The bitter events of Haymarket were followed, over the next few years, by more antilabor actions that firmly confirmed Chicago workers' belief in an ongoing collusion between the government and the business community. Many of the businessmen in the outlying townships who supported annexation in 1889, workers believed, had done so because they hoped that the Chicago police force would be a stronger deterrent against strikes and demonstrations than their limited local forces could ever be.

Five years later, in 1894, Chicago workers again confronted the determination of business to use the government to further its ends. In that year, workers struck George Pullman's huge car works at the south end of the city to protest pay cuts that were not accompanied by a reduction in rent and bills in their company-owned housing and stores. The strikers originally gained the sympathy of many Chicagoans, and neither Mayor Hopkins nor Illinois Governor John Altgeld was inclined to use force against them. But as the strike expanded to include attacks on any railroads using Pullman cars, a number of initially sympathetic Chicagoans, including a few newspapers, withdrew their support from the strikers. Hopkins and Altgeld remained reluctant to move against the strikers but Pullman and the railroads found an ally in the federal government. Under the pretext of protecting the federal mail delivery, President Cleveland's attorney general dispatched federal troops from nearby Fort Sheridan. When these forces met stiff resistance from strikers and their supporters, they were reinforced with additional troops from other states. With federal troops and federal marshalls "riding shotgun" on the trains, the strike was finally crushed.[38]

In the wake of the discouraging defeats suffered by the labor radicals, many of Chicago's organized workers joined the Chicago Federation of Labor (CFL). For many of these workers, the strongest lessons learned from Haymarket and Pullman were that they could not trust many of their fellow citizens and that they could not expect active sympathy for their causes from their municipal government as constituted. Acutely aware of its lack of power within the city, the CFL became an organization dedicated not only to protecting its members in the workplace, but also to providing them information on all municipal affairs and urging them to work to change the city's government.

Temperance was also a controversial issue in Chicago, and during the late nineteenth century it too played an important role in the development of Chicago's political culture. In 1839 the state legislature had enacted a statewide law regulating tavern licenses. Downstate counties had favored the measure while Chicago's representatives voted against it. From that time forward, the majority of Chicagoans had opposed prohibition and ardently fought attempts of prohibitionists to regulate more stringently the sale of liquor in the city.

As an issue, prohibition increased in importance as immigrants from cultural backgrounds where liquor played an important role in recreational activities poured into the city. Despite the overwhelming tolerance among Chicagoans for the sale of liquor, prohibitionists held a few strongholds within the city itself. This happened because, in the late 1880s, the city council had guaranteed the temperance forces that the dry township districts would not be eliminated when they were annexed into the city.[39] An uneasy truce between the two sides prevailed for a few years within the city despite the fact that Chicago consistently failed to enforce the state liquor laws, a fact that enraged the "drys." But the truce collapsed in 1893 when the Columbian Exposition opened in the "dry" Hyde Park section of the city. Outraged that the exposition's board of directors had secured a temporary liquor license for the fair, the prohibition forces revived their efforts both to bring the municipal government in line with the state liquor laws and to create more dry districts within the city.[40] Although the state incorporation act gave local legislatures power to license, regulate, and prohibit the sale of liquor, they had to do so within the strictures of state laws. One such law forbade liquor to be served after 1:00 A.M., while another—whose legal status was being contested—mandated the Sunday closing of all saloons. Neither law was being enforced in Chicago, and the Law and Order and Anti-Saloon Leagues began to insist that the city enforce these laws.

In an attempt to forestall conflict over the enforcement of these laws, which were wildly unpopular in the city, the city council sought a compromise measure. In March 1906, it doubled the saloon license fees to $1000, claiming that this measure would force disreputable saloons out of business and thereby help to eliminate vice in the city—one of the professed aims of the prohibitionists. At the same time, the council pointed out, the additional revenues could be directed toward fighting crime and vice in the city. The leagues were not mollified by the coun-

cil's compromise, and they received strong support from State
Attorney John Healy. Healy stepped into the fray and threatened to impeach Mayor Dunne if he did not enforce the state law
on 1:00 A.M. closings. Dunne was caught in a difficult situation.
He was an opponent of prohibition but the legal position of the
city was by no means certain. Therefore, he asked the council to
stop issuing the special bar permits that allowed clubs and dance
halls to serve liquor after that time. The council complied with
his request.[41]

There was a tremendous uproar in the city over both the increased license fee and the new ordinance restricing the special
permits. In late March, thirty thousand people representing
many of the city's ethnic groups assembled in a mass protest
meeting. Speakers warned the assembly that a small group of
prohibitionists within the city was conspiring with temperance
groups throughout the state to force prohibition on Chicago. To
forestall this event, they urged their audience to secure home-
rule powers for the city. Such powers, the speakers explained,
would guarantee that the people of Chicago could defeat any
state law by which "bigots attempt to subjugate the majority."[42]

The German newspapers of the city seized this idea. Two
months later, they issued invitations to ethnic groups throughout the city to attend a meeting with the purpose of organizing a
new society through which they could explore the possibilities of
securing home rule and become more closely involved in municipal affairs in general. In late May 1906, nearly 350 ethnic societies representing sixty thousand people responded to this
invitation and sent delegates to the founding meeting of the
United Societies for Local Self-Government.[43] This event was
soon going to have profound consequences for the new charter
movement. "Local self-government" meant municipal home rule,
and this issue emerged within the year as one of the fundamental and most controversial issues of charter reform.

On each of the three issues described—state-city relations,
labor problems, prohibition—the same groups of people within
Chicago tended to stand together. Immigrants and foreign-stock
residents and the workers who formed the bulk of the city's
population opposed prohibition, distrusted the business community, and were extremely wary of the state legislature. There

was certainly an element of class consciousness in their stance and in their later responses to the charter campaign, and it would be wrong to suggest otherwise. But it is important to understand what these people actively did with their class consciousness. How did they use it to try and reshape the city in ways desirable to them? How did their consciousness influence the positions they adopted on charter reform? Such questions are often overlooked in the study of the roles played by these urban residents in the reform movements of the early twentieth century.

The fourth and final element that had shaped Chicago's political culture by the end of the nineteenth century was the struggle over who in the city spoke for reform and what kind of reform. It is this element that also furnishes a starting point from which to begin exploring the development of changing ideas about urban life among Chicagoans of all kinds. Beginning in the 1870s with the Citizens' Association, various residents had banded together in civic organizations with the intent of reforming municipal affairs. The Citizens' Association functioned as a self-declared "watchdog" of municipal government. Its members monitored city-council actions and the growing problems of municipal taxation and administration and among themselves discussed and proposed possible changes in the way the city was governed. The Citizens' Association was a fairly typical reform group of its time: its members were generally businessmen who believed in fiscal responsibility and honesty in municipal government and thought it the business of government to provide a modestly congenial environment for business enterprise. The members of the association definitely did not believe that it was the business of government to get involved in financing social reform or to provide for the welfare of urban residents.

In the last decade of the century, two new civic groups, the Civic Federation and the Municipal Voters League, were founded. Both of these groups sympathized with the endeavors of the Citizens' Association, but they were organized by people whose views about the purposes of urban government were starting to diverge from those of the Citizens' Association. The Civic Federation came to life after a speech given in Chicago in 1893—the year that not only presented the Columbian Exposition, but also saw the country in the midst of a severe economic depression—by William T. Stead, an English editor and reformer. Stead castigated the city for its political corruption and government failures, but he also excoriated Chicagoans for what he believed was their callous treatment of the poor and unemployed. Many Chicagoans were stung by Stead's criticism, which he elaborated more fully in his book *If Christ Came to Chicago*, published soon afterward. In response to this "indictment of Chicago," as Jane Addams called it, a group of Chicago residents founded the Civic Federation. Its original members numbered businessmen, social workers, labor leaders, and socially prominent women. The foremost aim of the Civic Federation was to promote honest and economical government and tax reform, but founding members also professed the desire to use the organization to promote harmony between social classes and to ameliorate social ills.[44] Not only did these latter goals differ significantly from those of the Citizens' Association, they also revealed a shift of attitude toward the proper role of government: by focusing attention on social problems, members of the Civic Federation were beginning to flirt with the notion that ameliorating social ills was a proper function of municipal government.

The reactions of the Civic Federation to the Pullman strike, in the year after its inauguration, provide an example of shifting attitudes. While the city's leading businessmen—led by George Pullman, a long-time member of the Citizens' Association—petitioned Governor Altgeld and President Cleveland to send troops to break the strike, the Civic Federation sought to secure arbitration of the workers' grievances. The aim of the businessmen was to protect the rights of business against labor; that of the Civic Federation was to try to mediate the dispute in ways acceptable to both sides. However, even though some members of labor belonged to the Civic Federation, the organization and its stance on the Pullman strike can not be assessed as prolabor. Rather, the Civic Federation followed a new course shaped by its belief that social and labor grievances ought not to be solved by force or neglect because such means would inevitably prove detrimental to the city as a whole.

This was indeed a shift away from the more narrow urban

view of the Citizens' Association, but it is important not to exaggerate the Civic Federation's ideas at this point. Working with a Civic Federation committee established to help the unemployed during the prevailing economic depression by paying them to clean city streets, Jane Addams discovered just how limited this changing conception was. She was driven to despair by her inability to convince her co-workers to accept a broader, more long-term view of the situation of the working class and the problems of unemployment. She insisted "that it was better to have the men work half a day for seventy-five cents than a whole day for a dollar. . . . We must treat the situation in such wise that the men would not be worse off when they returned to their normal occupations." When her pleas fell on uncomprehending ears, Addams resigned from the committee.[45]

Furthermore, the Civic Federation's flirtation with social democracy did not survive the Pullman strike. Indeed, it is easy to see that this had not been a deep-felt ideal. Banker Lyman Gage, a founding member of the Civic Federation, rebuffed the request of two prominent Chicago women for a contribution to a worker's relief committee, saying that he admired "George Pullman and his town and that he would not hurt him in any way."[46] After the Civic Federation failed to secure arbitration of the Pullman strike, its more social-minded members resigned. Thenceforth, the Civic Federation directed its energies toward stemming civic corruption and reforming municipal taxation.

The second new organization of the decade was the Municipal Voters League, established in 1896. The MVL, too, viewed municipal problems in a somewhat different light than the Citizens' Association. Its members moved beyond the investigatory techniques of the Citizens' Association into taking direct political action. The older group had contented itself with researching and compiling records on officeholders. Until the last decade of the century, this had meant that anyone who was interested could go to the Citizens' Association and find out "who is in the public service, what different political offices or jobs he has held, and what his different positions in the political organizations have been. . . . If he has held an administrative office . . . it [the Citizens' Association] will hand you a box of newspaper clippings concerning the administration of that office."[47] But the

Citizens' Association itself had shunned direct political action. It assumed instead that its task was the more benign one of investigating and providing information for its members and like-minded citizens to use, but not involving itself directly in municipal politics. The Municipal Voters League, on the other hand, took the Citizens' Association's findings and used them to work for and against candidates for municipal office.

Viewing the city and its government in a broader perspective, the MVL acknowledged that since most of the male population voted on political candidates the only effective means of controlling and reforming urban government was to inform all the citizenry about issues and candidates.[48] The members of the MVL were able to arrive at this idea only after having first constructed a broader vision of the ramifications of urban politics. They first had to realize that they alone could neither reform nor control the city by assembling reports for "interested" parties to look at. Only then could these men move beyond investigation and into actual political campaigning, not the other way around.

A third new civic reform group appeared early in the first decade of the new century. This was the City Club of Chicago. The City Club was the idea of several members of the MVL who, in late 1903, believed that further city-wide reform required a broader municipal forum than was possible with any of the older organizations. Hence, the main function of the City Club was to provide a place where reform-minded citizens could participate in discussions on urban topics and urban problems. These discussions would then be published and theoretically accessible to everyone in the city. Lest anyone seek too democratic a stance for the City Club, however, its membership was strictly controlled. One could not apply for membership but had to be invited by a board of directors because, as one founding member explained it, membership was to be "confined to those who are sincerely interested in practical methods of improving public conditions."[49]

Despite this proliferation of reform organizations, the same group of men tended to be members of all three of the new organizations. Because they thereby talked primarily to themselves, they believed that the impulse toward urban reform came exclusively from within their ranks. Within such a context, it was easy for them to assume that all reform in the city should be guided by them. Thus, when the issue of charter reform arose, these men had become so accustomed to thinking that they spoke for the whole city when they spoke about reform, that most of them remained forever unable to comprehend that there could be other legitimate points of view.

The evidence left by the civic groups is abundant, and so many of their members played a prominent part in a broad range of municipal affairs that urban historians have often assumed that these men (the assumption does not include women) were in fact the only people in the city who had developed a "cosmopolitan" urban vision by the turn of the century. That this cosmopolitanism was seen as limited to this group of urban residents was implied by its narrow definition and explanation for its appearance. The cosmpolitan vision was viewed as coming from a "new recognition of the way in which factors throughout the city affected business growth."[50]

But from the late 1890s, there were other people in Chicago who proposed different solutions to the city's growing municipal problems. Two organizations dedicated to countering the proposals of the Civic Federation, MVL, and City Club were the Independence League and the Municipal Ownership League (MOL). In their aims, the members of these two organizations exhibited every bit as broad an urban vision as the "mainstream" reform organizations. Their vision, however, emanated from a different conception of good city government. Members of the Independence League and MOL believed that as businessmen and supporters of large corporations, those men who considered themselves the voice of reform in the city were in reality helping to create many of the worst municipal problems. The Independence League accused these men of perpetuating Chicago's chronic shortage of municipal revenues. According to the Independence League, the city lost every year millions of dollars in revenue that could have been used to provide and upgrade municipal services. This was so, the league charged, because businessmen saw to it that the corporations and the wealthy never paid their fair share of taxes. It is all too easy to dismiss these charges as political rhetoric. There was in fact a great deal of truth to these charges, as became quite apparent during the course of the new charter campaign when the question of who was supposed to pay for municipal improvements developed into a nasty issue.

There were many Chicagoans who were taking an avid interest in municipal affairs even though they were not members of these civic or reform groups. Women, for instance, were becoming more and more insistent upon playing a role in determining the future directions of the city. In the mid-1870s, several prominent Chicago women who were seeking to be "socially useful" founded the Chicago Woman's Club. But from this limited beginning, the club members quickly broadened the scope of their concerns to motives based less on social usefulness and more on an understanding of municipal problems. Even many of their earliest activities—sponsoring the appointment of a woman to the board of education and a woman doctor to the county insane asylum, helping establish kindergartens in the public schools, and supporting the activities of the Women and Children's Protective League—were based on the presumption that these were city-wide issues. As such, their resolution would affect the whole city, not just women and children.[51]

As they came to see the issues in which they were involved more and more in terms of their city-wide nature, the type of actions undertaken by the clubwomen changed. Their involvement with the problems of working women provides an example of this. First, the clubwomen concentrated on investigating and attacking specific cases of poor working conditions for women. They published a devastating exposé of working conditions during the Christmas rush at Marshall Field's and other major department stores in the city and supported the Chicago teachers in their fight for a pension fund. But it was not long before many of these women began to perceive that piecemeal reforms were not enough. This realization took them in the direction of aligning themselves with more far-reaching organizations such as the Women's Trade Union League and the Illinois Women's Alliance.[52]

At the same time, women throughout the city who had formed themselves into neighborhood clubs were discovering that the individual neighborhood problems they had set out to attack—clean streets, better garbage collection, and improved sanitary and health conditions—were in fact municipal problems that could not be effectively attacked piecemeal. One could not improve garbage disposal and sanitary conditions if indifferent landlords who did not live in the neighborhood refused to furnish adequate garbage receptacles or to maintain their property, as Jane Addams and the women of the Hull House neighborhood soon discovered.[53] Writing just a few years later, Addams recalled that the residents of settlement houses were "bound to regard the entire life of their city as organic, to make an effort to unify it, and to protest its overdifferentiation."[54]

Perceiving problems as interrelated and municipal in scope meant devising strategies of action different from the earlier reliance on volunteerism. Although it initially established and paid for nurses in the public schools, the board of the Visiting Nurses Association prided itself on convincing "the city, by practical illustration, that school nurses were necessary and to make the city assume the responsibility."[55] Working women also adopted new strategies. Catherine Goggins and Margaret Haley organized the predominantly female elementary school teachers into the Chicago Federation of Teachers in 1897. The federation's initial purpose was to fight the board of education's threats to suspend their three-year-old pension fund. The teachers won this fight, but the next year the board tried to regain the upper hand by withdrawing the first salary raise the teachers had received since 1877. Instead of attacking the board solely over this measure by demanding their right to the pay raise, the leaders of the CFT countered the board's arguments that it did not have the revenue by suing the city government to collect unpaid public utility taxes.[56] The CFT sought a municipal solution to a municipal problem: it devised a campaign that reflected its understanding of the direct connection between the board's refusal to raise teacher pay and municipal waste and corruption.

To portray the CFT's actions in this case as an example of interest-group mentality misses a valuable opportunity to see urban women working to understand the city as a whole. They were indeed taking a stand to protect their interests; but how they had come to define their interests, and what they thought their interests were—these are the important elements here. The teachers' awareness of past events and past history in the

city pushed them to see the interconnections between their plight
and the city's municipal problems. The members of the CFT realized that if one sector of the municipal government did not run
well, it affected the affairs of other sectors—that the parts would
not function adequately if the whole did not function well. When
the women of the CFT subsequently adopted other positions regarding the school system—favoring an elected board of education and public referenda on school issues, among other things—
they again did not act merely to protect jobs and pensions. They
believed that the way in which the public school system was constructed and to what ends it functioned, would determine the
quality and opportunity of life within the city for the future, not
just for themselves, but for the everyone in the city.[57]

In a variety of ways then, women in Chicago translated a
city-wide identity by gender into an understanding of metropolitan issues. Perhaps the most important aspect of the "municipal
housekeeping" movement of the Progressive Era was that it was
municipal: it encompassed a vision of the city as a whole in its
endeavors.[58] With that vision as a guiding principle, Chicago
women believed that their desired changes could be achieved
only if they had the power to determine change as a whole. For
this, they needed the municipal vote. From the late nineteenth
century, therefore, the energies of clubwomen, working women,
settlement-house women, and even immigrant women in Chicago were turned toward this end.[59] The vote, for all of them, became a way of controlling the entire urban environment in order
to restructure it along better lines.

Thus, the contours of Chicago's political culture had taken
shape before the new charter campaign. To see how Chicagoans
worked within their political culture before that issue became
the central one of the municipal reform movement, one may look
at the franchise issue. Franchise reform does not readily lend
itself to a tidy interest-group breakdown. Outside of Charles
Yerkes, his fellow franchise entrepreneurs, and a few remaining
diehards in the city council and legislature, it would have been
hard to find too many Chicagoans at the turn of the century who
did not favor franchise reform. Rather, the point in conflict was
how to reform the franchise system. The positions and rhetoric

advanced by opposing sides revealed clearly that what each side had was a different vision of the city as a whole and of the ways in which it should work. A synopsis of the history of franchise reform also provides the opportunity to see the impact that two of the components of Chicago's political culture—the past history of antagonism between city and state and between workers and businessmen—had on municipal issues.

Probably the last straw for the city on the franchise issue was the scandal of the Allen Bill in the late 1890s. In 1895, Yerkes had persuaded his friends in the state legislature to extend several of his traction franchises for ninety-nine years without his having to pay any further compensation to the city. Governor Altgeld vetoed this measure; but two years later, the legislature passed the Allen Bill, authorizing the city council to grant streetcar franchises for terms up to fifty years, replacing the prevailing twenty-year limit. Several of Yerkes' franchises expired in 1903, so he was particularly anxious to receive these extensions. He urged his remaining friends in the city council to move quickly in this regard, but before they could do so, outraged Chicago voters defeated all their state legislators who had voted for the Allen Bill. The city council took the hint and denied Yerkes' request.[60]

Following this episode, the clamor for franchise reform came from everywhere in the city. However, there was fundamental disagreement over how to accomplish such reform. The members of the Civic Federation and the MVL, believing in the primacy and efficacy of private business, wished to go about it by placing more restrictions on franchises granted to private companies. To their minds, once the cabal of dishonest businessmen and grafting politicians had been defeated by good laws and honest citizens, the franchise system itself would function quite well. The Independence League, Municipal Ownership League, Chicago Federation of Labor, and other groups in the city promoted instead total municipal ownership of public utilities.

By the end of the century, the conflicting ideas and aims of these citizens had manifested themselves in Chicago's political campaigns. In 1899, ex-governor John Altgeld ran for mayor and fielded a slate of candidates for city council on a reform platform that advocated immediate municipal ownership and fare reductions on public transit. William Kent, of the Municipal Voters League, asked Altgeld and his candidates to withdraw and support the MVL-backed candidates and their platform, who pledged a moderate reform position on franchises. Altgeld steadfastly refused to do so. The executive secretary of his campaign explained that they could not support the MVL candidates because of the profound differences between the reform ideas of the two groups. "While they [the MVL] are scratching the surface in the attempt to reform things, we are trying to strike at the root of the evil."[61] In other words, for the Altgeld people, the franchise system itself was the problem, and no amount of reform could possibly change that.

Altgeld lost the campaign to the regular Democratic candidate, Carter Harrison. But the municipal ownership issue had inserted itself into Chicago politics and it could not be removed. The issue played an important role in the mayoral campaigns of 1903, 1905, and 1907. In 1903, the question was most urgent because existing franchises were due to expire and a bill to allow cities to own and operate public transit systems was stalled in the legislature. The incumbent Mayor Harrison and his Republican challenger both endorsed this municipal ownership bill. However, Harrison went a step further and promised to veto any franchise extensions granted by the council before the law could be enacted. The voters reelected Harrison, and a month later, the legislature passed the Mueller Law, which empowered cities to build or buy and operate streetcar lines. To the dismay of municipal ownership advocates, Harrison proved not to be one of their number. He viewed the Mueller Law as a tool to force existing transit companies to renegotiate franchises more agreeable to the city, and he authorized the city council to begin franchise renegotiations even before the public referendum on the Mueller Law was held.

By doing this, Harrison turned his back on municipal ownership and refused to aknowledge the need for one unified transit system.[62] His outraged opponents succeeded in pushing up the referendum date and in placing two public-policy questions to test further the sentiment of the voters toward municipal ownership on the same ballot. Chicago voters passed the Mueller Law by more than the required three-fifths margin and gave overwhelming support to the other two propositions, one of which urged the council immediately to begin acquiring ownership of the traction companies under the terms of the Mueller Act.[63] Despite this evidence of citizen support for municipal ownership, Harrison stuck to his course.

Fortunately for the backers of municipal ownership, mayors then held office only for two years, and so in 1905 they had another opportunity to elect someone more supportive of their cause. Harrison declined to stand for another term, thereby making their task easier. The Democrats nominated Edward F. Dunne, who promised to implement immediate municipal ownership. Dunne was elected, and the voters registered overwhelming disapproval of the tentative traction ordinance that Harrison and the city council had negotiated.[64] Dunne, however, proved as disappointing as Harrison, for, despite his campaign pledge, he appointed Walter Fisher as his adviser on traction. A prominent civic reformer and member of the MVL and City Club, Fisher was a self-professed moderate on the question of traction reform. He did not favor municipal ownership, but rather urged Dunne and the city council to continue on their course of reform through renegotiation of existing franchises.

The ideological conflicts between these differing ideas on traction reform cannot be underestimated. Whether franchises were merely more tightly regulated or whether the government actually ran the public services would profoundly affect Chicago's urban environment. Anyone who has observed municipally owned public transit in European cities, where it is simply taken for granted now that it is the function of a municipal government to provide affordable and adequate mass transit, can attest to this.[65] Louis Post, newspaper editor, lawyer, and independent reformer, declared that there would never be, could never be, adequate municipal services as long as the public systems were in the hands of "private moneygrubbing corporations." If municipal services were conceived of as profit-making enterprises, he believed, the fundamental emphasis would always be on maximizing profits, rather than on providing the best possible public services with reasonable fares.[66] Moreover, the past experiences of Post and other proponents of municipal ownership, especially the Chicago Federation of Labor, did not give them any reason to trust the motives and ideas of those men backing franchise reforms. Not only had businessmen made it perfectly clear that they considered the business of the city to be business, the MVL, with its moderate stand on franchise reform, was led by William Kent, the son of a wealthy meat packer and stockholder in a private Chicago traction company![67]

One of the reasons why many Chicagoans were unwilling to compromise on this issue was precisely because it did involve conflicting visions of a good urban environment and municipal government. Two years after Dunne's election, the question of municipal ownership versus moderate franchise reform returned to bedevil the 1907 mayoral election campaign. Simultaneously, it affected the writing of the new charter and the charter ratification campaign that got underway shortly thereafter.

The experiences undergone within the city's political culture before the new charter was written would haunt and ultimately prove fatal to the entire charter reform movement. The differing ideas about how to resolve municipal problems that had already begun to develop within the city by the turn of the century could not be kept out of the charter campaign. Moreover, the traditions of political activism within the city meant that no small group or organization of citizens ever dominated Chicago's charter reform movement. By point of comparison here, small groups of citizens in other cities, sometimes in connivance with the state legislature, were often able to control charter reform to their own advantage. In New York City, for example, the charter of 1897 was drawn up by a small commission appointed by the state governor. The members of this commission believed it their mission "to produce a document that would satisfy the interested elite political and commercial groups" in the city. In this task they succeeded.[68] In Chicago, however, the movement to reform the municipal charter was a broad one in which all the citizens were able to participate at some point or another. Much to their chagrin, the hard-working members of the Civic Federation, Municipal Voters League, and City Club found that they were never able to avoid the affects of their city's political culture.

THE BEGINNINGS OF CHARTER REFORM

That conflicting visions of urban life might exist among the residents of Chicago at the turn of the century was not a fact acknowledged by the men who had begun to push for charter reform. These men thought of and spoke of themselves as reformers whose only goal was the good of the whole city. Thinking of themselves in this fashion, they viewed all reform proposals as a contest between reformers and nonreformers. In their self-righteousness, they labeled any opponents as selfish, corrupt, or narrow-minded; and they viewed the contest over charter reform in exactly this manner.

Historians have often simply taken the "reformers'" word for this situation. As a consequence, historians have discussed urban progressive reform movements in terms of this struggle between reformers and nonreformers. In doing so, they have created two problems that obscure our understanding of these movements. The first of these problems stems from the difficulties posed by relying on terminology to give meaning to a situation. In their research over the past twenty years, urban historians have continually found individuals or groups of city residents who seemed to be reformers, or called themselves reformers, but who did not fit neatly into the established definition of reformers. As a consequence, they have had to make the definition of *reformer* very elastic, expanding its meaning until the very word *reformer* was rendered essentially useless. Unless a taxonomy has an agreed-upon meaning as to the characteristics of those things placed within it, it is a false category. Second, by concentrating on discovering reformers, historians have not investigated closely the interactions of a broad spectrum of urban residents on crucial municipal issues to see what they can tell us of the context of urban reform in the Progressive Era.

For Chicago, the proposal for a new municipal charter that would free the city from the control of the state legislature and restructure the municipal government was just such an issue. The existing administrative and financial restraints under which the city was chafing by the turn of the century have already been detailed. This chapter will examine the beginnings of the new charter movement and the ways in which Chicago's context, its political culture, and the changing ideas about city life that can be seen taking form among its residents affected the movement right from its start.

Proposals to revamp Chicago's governing and taxing structure had surfaced from time to time in the late nineteenth century. In 1884, the Citizens' Association had recommended a series of constitutional amendments to accomplish this restructuring. But the Illinois Constitution barred the legislature from considering more than one amendment per session and the prospect of submitting and ratifying a number of amendments generated little enthusiasm among either Chicago residents or state legislators. By 1897, members of the Civic Federation had decided that the entire legal relationship between Chicago and Illinois was itself a major cause of Chicago's problems. The organization concluded, therefore, that something more than a series of constitutional amendments was needed to bring relief to the city. The existing legal system, it believed, was so cumbersome, inefficient, inequitable, and increasingly harmful to the city that it would have to be changed before meaningful urban reform could be accomplished. Thus, the Civic Federation made the reform of this legal relationship one of its primary goals.

Across the country, other urban residents, generally members of civic organizations resembling the Civic Federation, had likewise come to resent the role of the state government in municipal affairs. They objected to the inflexibility of state laws that kept cities from dealing efficiently with their own problems. They also resented what they were increasingly certain was the wanton interference by state legislators, and their often total disregard for municipal affairs. Thus, by the 1890s many concerned citizens had fastened upon municipal home rule as the general solution to the problems of urban government. In Chicago, the Civic Federation eagerly adopted this idea of home rule, pledging itself to work "until full control over all legislation affecting local interests is removed from the State Capitol to the city of Chicago."[1]

Although the Civic Federation leaned toward obtaining home rule through writing a new charter, this means for securing municipal reform was certainly not agreed upon within the city. In 1899, a group of businessmen proposed that the consolidation of overlapping taxing and governing authorities would solve the most pressing of Chicago's problems. Meeting as the Greater Chicago Committee, they proposed a single amendment to extend the city limits to include all of Cook County and subsume all functions of county government under the city. Their proposal failed to attract much enthusiasm; but the prospect of such a consolidation appealed to many Chicago residents, including members of the Civic Federation, who were daily growing more concerned about the county government's influence over municipal revenues. In 1901, Mayor Carter Harrison adopted this idea of consolidation and moved to undercut the role of the citizenry in any such reform by asking the city council to recommend constitutional amendments enabling the city to consolidate all existing taxing bodies under the municipal government. When it became apparent to him that sentiment in the city was shifting away from separate amendments toward securing a new municipal charter from the state, Harrison quickly changed his position and suggested to the council members that as the "legally authorized representatives of Chicago," they should take the lead in this matter.[2] The aldermen agreed. They passed a resolution empowering Harrison to appoint a council committee on state legislation whose duty was to report back to the council by January 1, 1903, with recommendations on what was needed "for the proper government of Chicago and Cook County."[3]

The politicians' attempt to usurp the role of citizens' groups in directing charter reform galvanized the members of the Civic Federation, most of whom were neither Harrison Democrats nor admirers of the mayor, into immediate action. Within a month, the Civic Federation invited "influential" groups to send delegates to a convention to discuss charter reform. In the meantime, the Civic Federation's ideas of municipal reform crystallized, and it prepared a report urging that a new municipal charter be written to redress both the cumbersome legal status of the city and restructure the governing and taxing authority of the municipal government. The Civic Federation called for such a charter to consolidate overlapping governing bodies within the municipal boundaries, extend the allowable debt limit for cities, reform the structure and powers of the Chicago City Council, and in general make it easier for the city to expand governmentally and geographically.[4]

Thus, on October 28, 1902, seventy-four men from the city's leading business and social clubs, civic organizations, political groups, and a few delegates-at-large assembled as the Chicago New Charter Convention. The Chicago *Tribune*, a vigorous supporter of the proceedings, described the convention as "a really representative body. There is no prominent organization, municipal, individual, or political which will not be represented." The *Tribune*'s definition of representation was somewhat narrow: the overwhelming majority of these men were successful businessmen and professionals; the Chicago Federation of Labor sent two delegates, but except for three men from Jewish business clubs, the city's ethnic population was underrepresented.[5] Obviously, the operative words for the *Tribune* and the Civic Federation were "prominent" and "influential." The failure to constitute a more representative convention resulted from the belief of these few men and their organizations that they themselves were the city's spokespersons for reform.

Having structured the convention, the Civic Federation felt secure in its leadership. Members of the organization assumed control of the convention from its first meeting. They told the assembled delegates that they had two legal means for securing charter reform: they could seek a new state constitution, or they could write an enabling amendment to the present document that would specifically allow Chicago to draft a new charter. The Civic Federation clearly favored the latter course. Its President, B. E. Sunny, opened the convention by reminding the delegates that forces outside of Chicago still controlled the state legislature and that these men did not want a new constitution. On the other hand, he pointed out, the legislators were unhappy with the continuous stream of amendments brought before them by Chicago—there were twenty-three such bills currently pending in Springfield—and seemed willing to agree to a new municipal charter for the city to alleviate the situation. Sunny encouraged the delegates to begin the task of securing a new charter for Chicago, because, as "men foremost in Chicago's business activities, skilled in the solution of difficult problems," they were best qualified for the job.[6]

The delegates concurred with the Civic Federation's assessment of the situation, and of themselves, and appointed a committee to draft an "enabling" amendment. Having adopted this strategy, the convention then charged the committee to decide also whether this amendment should be a simple grant of power to Chicago to write a charter, or whether the amendment itself should also specify the exact municipal powers the city wanted to include in any new charter.[7] It is evident in the record of the convention proceedings of this first meeting that the convention as a whole, and especially the Civic Federation, did not expect any opposition to its plans. In this feeling, they were supported by the *Tribune*. As confident of a general consensus about charter reform as it was of the convention's representativeness, the paper sternly admonished any potential opponents that their voice was not legitimate because a new charter involved "policy and not principle."[8]

Imbued thus with the certainty of its own position, the committee retired to write the amendment. Several weeks later, it reported back to the full convention a proposal that occupied a middle ground between vagueness and specificity: it gave the legislature power to provide a charter of local government for Chicago, but it did not confine itself to this simple authorization. Instead, the amendment embodied the Civic Federation's idea that consolidation and tax reform were the first priorities of municipal reform. The enabling amendment stipulated that any new charter should consolidate into the municipal government the powers currently held by the county, the board of education, the library board, the townships, and the park and sanitary districts and that once the city had consolidated with any two of these bodies it would be allowed to assume their debts and liabilities and thereby increase its level of legal indebtedness. With this consolidation scheme, the city's debt limit would have jumped from 1 to 5 percent, and it would have controlled the tax levies from the entire tax district instead of its current restriction to 2 percent of assessed property valuation.[9]

Consolidation and tax reform were exactly the reform measures that the Civic Federation wanted, and the enabling amendment reflected their precise desires. But when the committee reported this amendment back to the full convention, there was dissent. Some of the delegates did not agree with the *Tribune* that principle was not involved in charter reform. James Linehan, delegate from the CFL, objected to the vagueness of the amendment in certain respects: it did not specify who would write a new charter and it did not enumerate what new municipal powers were to be written into such a charter. Linehan argued that the amendment, as currently written, did not even guarantee that Chicago itself would get to write its new charter. What, he asked his fellow delegates, was to safeguard the city against losing control of the entire process and winding up with a charter drafted by the state legislators? Furthermore, he distrusted the motives behind the convention's refusal to draft a more specific amendment. He accused the delegates of duplicity by clearly spelling out the consolidation and taxation schemes they wanted in the charter, while they "ignored the will of the people and failed to include a clause endorsing initiative, referendum, and municipal ownership," all measures approved by Chicagoans in recent public-policy ballots. He also warned the convention that the CFL might refuse to support this amendment.[10]

Although Linehan received support for his objections from a few other delegates, the convention as a whole rejected a proposal that the amendment include a phrase specifically providing for municipal ownership in any new charter. Insisting that the legislature would only pass a vague general amendment allowing consolidation, the convention adopted the enabling amendment as written by the committee.[11] It might be argued that in light of the antagonism between city and state, the delegates were merely being prudent, but there are two strong objections to such an argument. First, there is no explicit evidence that the legislature was any more intrinsically open to the consolidation scheme than to municipal ownership, as will be seen throughout the rest of the charter campaign. Second, most of these men wanted consolidation, not municipal ownership. And because municipal ownership was a volatile issue within the city at the moment, the men running this convention had no intention of allowing it into the amendment. The legislature's possible hostility provided them, now and later, with a convenient excuse for overriding the objections of their opponents. To try to defuse this issue, the Civic Federation claimed that it was sufficient at this point to agree in theory to charter reform. Linehan and his supporters, on the contrary, argued that the type of charter reform to be undertaken did indeed matter and that the people were entitled to know what would result from a new charter before voting to authorize such legislation. Linehan's distrust of the state legislature and his businessmen colleagues at the convention, as well as his objections to the amendment itself, foreshadowed the conflicts that would plague the charter movement for the next five years.

Despite this conflict, the convention sent the amendment to the legislature supremely confident of its passage and of a future new charter for the city. They soon experienced their first setback. Although B. E. Sunny had been correct that the legislators generally favored a Chicago charter to relieve the burden of local legislation for Chicago, many of them wanted the reform on their terms and not Chicago's. Several "downstaters", led by representatives Bundy (Republican from Centralia) and Tippit (Democrat from Olney), representing what they termed the "country element," attempted to exchange the amendment for new state tax laws desired by downstate; and once again they demanded a permanent limit on the number of Chicago and Cook County representatives. "We are using this question as a club if you like," said Bundy.[12] The legislature made it perfectly clear to Chicago that it would do everything in its legal power to keep the city under its thumb even with a new charter. The downstaters did not succeed in either of these tactics, but their actions gave Chicagoans reason to fear similar tactics in the future, quite conceivably over the charter itself. Moreover, before it passed the enabling amendment, the legislature did make a substantive change. It limited the consolidation scheme to the city, the board of education, the library board, the townships, and the park districts. The county government and the sanitary district would remain separate governing and taxing bodies even under a new charter.[13]

Although this revision disappointed the Civic Federation and other proponents of charter reform, they accepted the amendment, arguing that it still allowed enough consolidation and tax reform to be worthwhile. They began preparations for submitting it to the required referendum of all Illinois voters. The supporters of the amendment were particularly anxious to obtain a large affirmative vote in Chicago to offset what they feared would be mass negative voting in the rest of the state. The Civic Federation was also most anxious to maintain control of the charter movement and, early on, beat back another challenge to its position by Mayor Harrison and the city council. Attempting to bring the issue under control of the municipal government, the council authorized Harrison to appoint from its membership a special Chicago Charter Amendment Campaign Committee with power to take whatever steps it deemed necessary to promote adoption of the amendment. Once constituted, the committee was authorized to invite the cooperation of civic organizations and form an auxiliary committee of citizens under its aegis to assist in educating Chicago voters on behalf of the amendment. The Civic Federation refused to relinquish its prominent role in the campaign. Although it cooperated with the council committee, its own New Charter Campaign Committee remained the most vocal and active promoter of the amendment. Through this

committee, the Civic Federation disseminated literature throughout the city, urging voters to ratify the amendment on the
grounds that Chicago's first reform priority was to free itself
from the restraints of the Cities and Villages Act.[14]

As James Linehan had predicted, the Civic Federation's determination to keep a firm hand on the charter reform movement along with the amendment itself made the CFL hesitant to
recommend that its membership ratify the amendment. Ratification of the Mueller Law in April 1904 defused the CFL's objection to the amendment's failure to ensure municipal ownership, but Harrison's renegotiation of the existing franchises, and
the strong stance against municipal ownership by the men supporting the amendment, left the CFL uncertain about the ad-
visability of supporting the amendment. Also, the organization
still objected to the amendment's emphasis on taxation and failure to specify other municipal reforms and to its vagueness on
who would write the new charter or how much home rule Chicago would obtain in such a document.

The CFL remained on the fence until the Civic Federation
pushed it off a few weeks before the November 1904 referendum
when the board of education gave the federation permission to
hold a "charter day" and distribute procharter information in
the schools. The CFL felt confirmed in its worst suspicions about
who would benefit from charter reform in its proposed format,
especially when the board denied to the CFL similar access to
the schools to promote the public policy questions on direct primary, popular veto, and local power to assess and levy taxes that
were to appear on the same ballot as the referendum. In the ensu-
ing uproar, the board canceled the Civic Federation's privilege;
but it was too little too late. The CFL's political action committee
denounced the amendment as an attempt by "every corporate
agent, every subsidized newspaper, and every lick-spittle syn-
cophant" to gain control of the city.[15] It felt even more justified in
its position, when, on the day of the referendum, the *Tribune*
boasted of how many of the largest merchants and manufacturers in the city had "lent" employees to help the campaign
committee during the final days of the campaign.[16]

Obviously, there was class conflict at work here. But why

should the CFL have trusted the motives behind reform proposals avidly backed by the leading businessmen of the city,
given the past history of labor relations within Chicago? Furthermore, the CFL's position regarding municipal ownership
possesses its own reform logic. The question of whether municipal governments should be vested with the power to own, operate, and provide extremely necessary public utilities was every
bit as vital an issue as what kind of taxing powers a government
should possess; and it was as much a part of a complete urban
vision as the ideas held by members of the Civic Federation or
the business community.

And the CFL did not stand alone at this juncture. Several of
the city's liberal independents, including Louis Post, spoke out
against the amendment. Along with the CFL, they proposed
that charter reform be undertaken instead by writing a new
state constitution. Post had no more trust in businessmen than
the CFL did, and he did not concur with the Civic Federation's
ideas about good municipal government. He argued that certain
"financial" interests opposed a new constitution, not because
state legislators would be against it, but because any constitutional convention would inevitably include groups antagonistic
to their desires. Watching the machinations of the Civic Federation, both Post and the CFL had come to believe that a constitutional convention would be the only way to ensure that the
people of the city would have a voice in how their city was to be
reformed.[17]

Serious objections to the amendment itself surfaced too late
to be of much consequence for the referendum. Chicago voters,
by and large, believed in the need for municipal reform and approved the amendment by a margin of ten to one among those
voting. A majority of voters in the state heeded their representatives' explanations that it would free the legislature from
an overload of requests for legislation from Chicago and also
ratified the amendment. Chicago was now legally able to secure
some type of new municipal charter, and the next steps in the
process were to decide how to accomplish this and to consider
what provisions a new charter should contain.

The overwhelming approval of the amendment by Chicago

voters may have produced more optimism among the amendment's strong backers about the future of charter reform than was warranted, given the prevailing political climate in the city. The last-minute, but decidedly bitter, opposition of the CFL should have warned them to expect more opposition from that quarter. There was also other evidence close at hand that while the majority might agree on the need for charter reform, they might genuinely disagree on the shape of that reform. The voting on the two public-policy questions which had shared the ballot with the amendment was one such indication. By a majority of ten to one, Chicagoans had approved the proposition that the citizens should be able to veto any undesireable action of their local government; and they had favored by over three to one the idea that local governments should be empowered to adopt their own system of assessing and levying taxes, subject to popular referendum.[18] Finally, the backers of the amendment should have realized from the battle over municipal ownership currently raging in the city that there was also no municipal consensus on this issue. These three measures, if ever enacted, were to bring to Chicago far more home rule, popular decision making, and direct government than the amendment's principal backers had ever suggested. Their popularity indicated that a sizeable number of Chicago residents held an entirely different conception of the proper scope and workings of a municipal government than that of the reformers of the Civic Federation.

In their euphoria over having won the battle for the amendment, however, the men leading the new charter campaign realized none of this. They more or less assumed that they would continue to have their way; and because the enabling amendment so conveniently provided no mechanism for deciding who would write a new charter, they set out to do it themselves. In late November of 1904, the extant executive committee of the 1902 convention named a new Committee of Seven to draft a charter, giving it no charge but to seek from the citizenry "such assistance as might be helpful."[19] In view of the concerns voiced at the convention and afterward about who would write the charter, the lack of any possible popular input into a charter so written could have been expected to cause a howl of protest from some quarters in the city. The particular seven men placed on this committee guaranteed that it would happen. Three of the men, John P. Wilson, Judge Francis Adams, and John S. Miller, were also members of that same executive committee. Miller, moreover, was special corporation counsel for the Union Traction Company, one of the franchise-holders currently engaged in resisting municipal ownership. Of the other four appointees, many Chicagoans were bound to object to three: B. E. Sunny, who was outgoing president of the Civic Federation; B. A. Eckhart, who was a prominent manufacturer and had represented the board of trade at the new charter convention two years earlier; and Mayor Carter Harrison, who was busily engaged in forestalling any attempts to bring about municipal ownership. Furthermore, Sunny, Miller, Wilson, and Eckhart all belonged to the Union League Club, where Sunny, in addition to presiding over the Civic Federation, was chairman of the club's political action committee.[20]

If the CFL suspected that certain business interests intended to dominate charter reform and if the forces behind municipal ownership feared that the new charter would be used to thwart their wishes, the composition of this Committee of Seven was all the confirmation they needed. The members of the Union League Club envisioned themselves as among the leading figures in charter reform, and they intended to remain influential. A few months before this, Merritt Starr, who sat on the club's political action committee along with B. E. Sunny, had written a letter to Sunny detailing the club's activities regarding charter reform. Of the seventy-one living delegates of that convention, he pointed out, thirty-two belonged to the Union League Club, and he added that "it is fair to say that the Union League Club has from the beginning held a leading place in the movement for City Charter Revision, and it desires to continue active in this work." In his letter, Starr also reminded Sunny of the club's objective to secure a charter "drawn on rational and scientific lines and utilizing to the upmost all of the lessons of experience and embodying no rash experiments which have no justification in experience at their back."[21] This Committee of Seven must surely have pleased Starr.

However, precisely as James Linehan had predicted at the 1902 convention, the issue of who would write the charter became a sharply contested matter. The CFL was infuriated at the thought of the Union League Club and Civic Federation controlling charter reform. It immediately offered counterproposals, first demanding that a specified number of men from organized labor be representatives to any new charter body. The CFL soon abandoned this stance in favor of a new plan that a 350-member, elected convention write a charter. According to this plan, all Chicago citizens (and only Chicagoans) would be eligible for membership in the convention, with delegates nominated by petition and elected at large by plurality vote. The CFL defended this plan as the only way to preclude the possibility of a charter convention controlled by one or two factions, which, of course, was exactly what the Union League Club and Civic Federation had had in mind.[22]

Because the enabling amendment had specified no mechanism for naming a body to write a charter, once objections were raised, the problem was not readily solvable or controllable. The old convention could name its Committee of Seven, but it had no authority of law to enforce it. The CFL was in the same bind. Therefore, despite its reluctance to deal with the state legislature, the CFL chose its only possible legal recourse and sent its proposal to the House and Senate charter committees, where it was immediately rejected. The legislature itself then tried its hand at constituting a charter convention. Representative John McGoorty (D-Chicago) introduced a bill to constitute a convention of ninety elected and twenty-five appointed members; but this bill and four others failed to pass the legislature, which was hopelessly at odds over how Chicago was to write a new charter.

With Chicago residents also at odds and no convention plan forthcoming from Springfield, the city council stepped into the breech in May 1905.[23] Democrats and Republicans in the council introduced separate plans for assembling a convention. The Republican plan, introduced by Alderman Milton Foreman, proposed a convention of seventy-four appointed delegates: fifteen city council members selected by the council itself, fifteen state legislators chosen by the presiding officers of each house, fifteen appointees each of Governor Deneen and Mayor Dunne (newly elected the month before), and two representatives each appointed by the board of cook county commissioners, trustees of the sanitary district, the board of education, the library board, and each of the three park boards. With the exception of Mayor Dunne and the library board, all of the appointing agents were controlled by the Republicans.[24]

Council Democrats cried foul and accused the Republicans of designing a Republican convention to ensure that certain provisions, such as municipal ownership, were not written into a new charter. Alderman Joseph Kohout countered the Foreman Plan with his own plan for appointing a convention of 110 delegates. Under the Kohout Plan, every city council member would appoint one delegate, five aldermen would be appointed by the Council Committee on State Legislation, Governor Deneen would make five appointments and Mayor Dunne fifteen, and each of the municipal governing boards would appoint two delegates. The Kohout Plan, unlike the Foreman Plan, also stipulated that all the delegates, except those appointed by the governing bodies, had to reside in Chicago.[25]

Beyond the mere fact of political party disagreement over who would write a new charter, there are three items about these plans, and the arguments over them, that are important to consider a bit further. The first is that, although each side claimed its plan as nonpartisan, obviously both Republicans and Democrats were attempting to shape a partisan convention. This is not surprising. However, all too often, historians have tended to take at face value the Republican reformers' claim to nonpartisanship. They were in fact highly partisan, because they believed that men just like them should control the convention in order to ensure that they got the charter they wanted. It is doubtful that there was anyone in Chicago who did not firmly believe that the finished charter would reflect the views of those who drafted it on the controversial issues such as home rule, municipal ownership, taxation, and schools. Second, the Kohout Plan did differ in two significant ways from the Foreman Plan. The Democrats' plan was seeking to ensure that those men responsible for drafting a new charter for the city were men who lived in the city, and, at the same time, it was trying to remove the state legislature entirely from the convention. The CFL, in its proposal for an elected convention, had been attempting to accomplish much the same thing. Third, in light of the municipal election just passed (April 1905), during which municipal ownership had once again been a most contested issue, the Democrats' objection that the Foreman Plan stacked the deck to ensure that at least sixty members of the convention would be against municipal ownership cannot be lightly dismissed as mere rhetoric.[26] Municipal ownership was on the minds of all Chicagoans in 1905, and they had every reason to believe that a new charter would have to solve the question one way or the other. Thus, which men sat in the charter convention would be a critical factor for Chicago's subsequent municipal development.

The Republicans held the majority in the council in 1905 and their ranks stayed firm in voting on the plans. The Foreman Plan therefore was adopted, and the various appointing agencies began making their selections. The resulting convention was every bit as Republican as the Democrats had predicted, and every bit as business-oriented as the CFL had feared.[27] Of the sixty-two delegates whose political affiliation are identifiable, thirty-nine were Republicans, twenty-two were Democrats, and one was an Independent. The city council named ten Republicans and five Democrats, eight of Governor Deneen's appointees were Republican, and only one of the state legislature's choices was a Democrat. The West and Lincoln park boards, whose members had been appointed by the governor, sent two Republicans each to the convention, while the "Democratic" library board sent two Democrats. Only Mayor Dunne appointed more Democrats than Republicans. By occupation, there were twenty-six lawyers, thirty-two businessmen, two social workers, one professor, and one minister. Many of these men were the same ones who had been active in the previous reform movements of the Civic Federation and Municipal Voters League. Even the few ethnic delegates were mostly well-to-do businessmen; only two delegates were members of the CFL, and one delegate was a black businessman. Mayor Dunne had appointed these last three members.

This representative imbalance was acknowledged neither by the convention itself, nor by historians who have studied the charter movement previously and who have simply taken the so-called reformers' word for it that the convention represented all the citizenry. The chairman of the convention, Milton Foreman, assured the city that "an inspection of the membership will disclose the fact that they represent every walk and condition and poll of thought in life."[28] In fact, little attempt had been made to constitute a convention that would represent all the people in the city. Even when some of the more fair-minded reformers considered the issue, they revealed a narrow concept of fair representation. For instance, when Governor Deneen sent to Walter Fisher a list of his tentative appointees, Fisher (who was on Deneen's list) suggested that the governor revise his list to include more groups within the city. He commended the governor's choice of Lessing Rosenthal, because he represented the Jewish element, and suggested that the governor match this with a "prominent" Catholic. Observing that the list overly represented the "conservative and property-owning element," Fisher proposed appointing "some representative of the labor or radical class." Fisher spoke in the singular: one Jew, one Catholic, one from the radical or labor element. The restricted nature of Fisher's idea of equal representation was further indicated by his suggestion of a man to represent the Germans and the liquor interests who was also general counsel and director of Republic Steel and Iron. Thus, as Fisher pointed out, he would also represent large manufacturers.[29]

What most concerned Fisher—and the preoccupation was shared by the other men prominent in the charter campaign—was that the right people with the right ideas be appointed to the convention. They were not anxious to have the convention be a popular, representative body. On the one hand, such political thinking is readily understandable; on the other hand, with the strenuous objections that other Chicagoans were raising against this type of limited convention, it would have been more politically astute to seek some better compromise at this point rather than to risk further alienating a sizeable portion of the citizenry before work on the new charter had even commenced.

Now, and throughout the remainder of the charter campaign, however, the men controlling the charter movement consistently underestimated the strength of opposition to them and their ideas and stubbornly refused to acknowledge that their opponents might indeed have ideas of their own about good charter reform.

THREE

THE CHARTER CONVENTION

Despite the signs that opposition was developing within the city to charter reform as the movement's leaders envisioned it, the delegates convened their first regular session on November 30, 1906, with great optimism. They had first met in two special sessions, one in July and another in early October, to draw up convention rules and constitute committees to begin studying the separate issues—among them the powers and duties of the mayor and city council, public education, public utilities, municipal election rules, parks, municipal home rule—that would be addressed by the new charter. Now they were ready to get down to work and hammer out the charter.

Their first deliberations, about changing the structure of the municipal government, present an interesting feature of Chicago's charter reform campaign: the delegates had little interest in centralizing the government along the lines being adopted elsewhere across the country. New charters in Boston and New York, for example, eliminated the council's power to increase municipal budgets and gave the mayor power to appoint and remove all department heads without council confirmation; Pittsburgh and Boston reduced the number of their city council members and introduced at-large elections to replace the old ward system of elections; many other cities reorganized entirely into very tightly centralized commission governments.[1]

But in Chicago, where the highly decentralized, city council and ward-based system had come under attack toward the end of the century for rampant corruption and inefficiency, charter reformers did not try to sweep away this nineteenth-century system of municipal government. They rejected a proposal made by delegate Alexander Revell for a modified at-large plan, wherein each ward would have nominated candidates for aldermen in a primary, after which the entire city would have selected from among the nominees of each ward. Beyond this, the most radical measure that the convention considered for reconstituting the city council was to reduce the number of aldermen. At the time, Chicago was divided into thirty-five wards, each sending two aldermen to the council; aldermen served for two-year terms, and half their number stood for election each year. Delegates B. A. Eckhart and R. R. McCormick proposed that a smaller council, either thirty-five or fifty wards with one alderman each, be created. Fewer aldermen, they argued, could more efficiently carry out the city's business because they would have to be more attentive to the whole city's needs, and less preoccupied with their individual wards. The majority of the delegates, however, remained firmly ward-oriented, insisting both that servicing the ward was a vital duty of aldermen and that the city could not operate efficiently with fewer representatives. But they accepted a compromise measure to redistrict the city into seventy wards with one alderman each.[2]

The reasons that these men did not push vigorously for a major overhaul of the existing aldermanic structure sprang directly from their personal political experience. Many of the most ardent proponents of charter reform believed that wholesale structural change was no longer necessary because the Municipal Voters League had already fought and won the war against corruption.[3] Delegate Charles Merriam, a professor of political science at the University of Chicago, reflecting back upon this

period sometime later, wrote that the reform crusades of the
MVL had "raised the Council to a cleaner and sounder basis . . .
and gave the City for twenty years the best local legislative body
in the country." Although a Republican himself, Merriam credited five-time Democratic mayor Carter Harrison for governing
Chicago with a political realism that kept the city from splitting
into hostile reform and non-reform camps, each struggling for
control of the council.[4] In this same vein, before the convention
had yet convened, delegate Walter L. Fisher wrote a correspon-
dent from Minnesota that he could "cite Chicago as a city where
nonpartisan municipal politics has been a practical success."
Lincoln Steffens in his famous expose of urban political corruption, even congratulated Chicagoans for beginning "slow,
sure, political, democratic reform, by the people, for the people,"
and concluded that there was "little doubt that Chicago will be
cleaned up."[5]

Strong words of praise from strange quarters, considering
the harsh criticisms that had been hurled at the "grey wolves" of
the Chicago City Council just a few short years before by such
men as Merriam and Fisher. Why did they adopt this position?
Merriam had tended always to be optimistic about the state of
municipal affairs in Chicago and continued to be fairly generous
in his assessments of political opponents even after they had defeated him.[6] It is Fisher's assessment that is the more interesting and revealing of what the promoters of charter reform were
thinking, and it gives a different impression of the reformers'
aims from that usually acknowledged. For what Fisher extolled
as nonpartisan government was in reality Republican party
government. The campaigns of the MVL had indeed thrown out
many of the "grey wolves," but they had also put the Republicans
in control of the council. When this first occurred in 1900, the
Republicans moved quickly to reconstitute council committees
along highly partisan lines. Despite its hitherto sacred nonpartisan pledge, the MVL readily concurred with this move, saying
that "it is understood . . . that most, even of the more prominent
reform members, do not regard the [nonpartisan] pledge as bind-
ing in the event it can be shown that better results can be accomplished by the majority party having control of the committees

and working machinery of the Council." MVL leader George Cole gave the new council and its maneuvers his imprimatur, saying it would be "the best governed municipality between the Atlantic and Pacific."[7]

Because so many of the ardent municipal reformers, those men belonging to the Civic Federation and Municipal Voters League, for instance, were also Republicans, once their party was in control, they became extremely reluctant to tamper with the existing political structure. Chicago's civic reform organizations certainly resembled greatly those in cities across the country, and the men who belonged to them spoke the same language of reform, advocating efficiency and nonpartisanship. But their major point of reference remained their own city.

Six years later, as the convention got underway, many of these men still felt enough in control of the political scene to express almost unbounded confidence that Chicago would continue to experience good government, even under its ward-based system. Part of understanding Chicago's charter movement thus is understanding that those men who considered themselves, and talked about themselves, as nonpartisan reformers, in fact were quite partisan. Because this was so, and because the term *nonpartisan* has been used generously by historians to explain the motives and aims of such men as these, the very use of the term *nonpartisan* should be greeted with skepticism. These men thought of themselves as nonpartisan because they themselves had defined their cause as nonpartisan politics. But their rhetoric did not necessarily reflect the political reality and practice, as a careful look at the charter movement and the political campaigns in the city in this time period shows.[8]

That the convention delegates were not interested in implementing new centralization techniques because they believed that the MVL had been so successful also reveals an aspect of Chicago's prevailing political culture that has not been systematically explored. The MVL's success in electing its approved candidates to the city council[9] suggests that political reform was not an unknown or unpopular quality among Chicagoans. The voters of Chicago were not simply possessed of a localist outlook, machine-oriented, uninterested in municipal reform, and content to let corrupt and graft-ridden aldermen run their city. The MVL could not have succeeded if large numbers of Chicago voters had not supported their cause.

However, the very success of their anticorruption campaigns and their vision of themselves as nonpartisan caused the men in the MVL and other civic organizations to make the mistake of assuming that because the voters generally agreed with them in this instance, they would agree wholeheartedly with them on a whole range of other reform issues thereafter.[10] They said so at the convention and at other times, consistently repeating the theme that everything would be fine because as long as the "reformers" did their job of informing the people of the correct position, then the electorate would vote the correct way.[11] But, by putting reform in these terms, these men, in their minds, set up a rigid dichotomy: either the voters were for them or against them, and there could be no such thing as differing ideas. Thus, while during the convention the delegates were complacent about not dismantling the old political mechanisms, many of these same men became exceedingly hostile and insulting toward their fellow citizens when ultimately they did not get their way on the charter.[12]

Once the delegates began debating the rest of the provisions for a new charter, the issues at stake provoked more controversy and more pressure from citizens outside the convention room. Although the convention was able to pass with little dissent the measure to renumber the wards and also a resolution to consolidate the municipal government, the park districts, the board of education and the library board, as allowed by the amendment of 1904, as soon as the delegates began debating how to distribute powers within this consolidated system, voices throughout the city were raised in protest. Thenceforth, the convention was inundated with petitions and constantly assailed by dissenting opinions from outside as well as inside its chambers. The text of the convention proceedings shows that Chicagoans of all types considered the charter convention to be a forum for expressing their ideas on municipal reform. But it also shows that the delegates themselves failed to take this situation seriously.

One of the first charter provisions to spark sharp disagreement was a proposal to lengthen aldermanic terms to four years.

The term of office was an important issue because consolidation would increase the taxing and decision-making powers of the council. One group of delegates, led by Walter Fisher, urged adoption of the four-year terms because they believed that it would increase efficiency: aldermen, they argued, needed sufficient time to assess municipal needs and problems and work out solutions, and two years was not enough time. Moreover, the convention had already increased the term of mayor to four years and political symmetry would be achieved if the whole municipal governing body served the same term. But opponents of this proposal, led by James Linehan of the CFL and Louis Post, protested that longer aldermanic terms would lessen popular representation. "The people can change their opinion inside of two years," Linehan argued. "As an expression of that change, they would change the great body of the aldermen, and that would be sufficient notification to the mayor that [a] policy is no longer desirable by the people. On the other hand, if [a] policy is desirable, and the aldermen are not supporting the mayor, there will be an opportunity for the people to send in someone that will support him." [13]

Those men who favored retaining the two-year term for aldermen lost this battle, however, as the convention voted to implement the longer term under the new charter. Their arguments for retaining the shorter term illustrate a differing, yet no less valid, view of good municipal government than that of the delegates backing the four-year term. This particular issue can be evaluated from two perspectives. The first is to see these conflicting positions in the context of the city's past. It was neither from accident nor shortsightedness that the most prominent spokesperson for popular representation on this issue, and on other charter issues to come, was a member of the CFL. Based on past experience, James Linehan and his fellow workers in the city had no reason whatsoever to trust the motives of businessmen. Linehan had no doubt that when the businessmen-delegates extolled efficiency and good municipal administration as being best accomplished by a few for the good of the whole city, they were conveniently equating the good of the city with what was good for them.

The second perspective derives from treating urban reform

as a process in which large numbers of the urban population were coming to view themselves as part of the whole community and assessing how best to reorganize and control this community. In such a context, it is possible to see that conflict over an issue like this did not involve efficiency versus machine politics or cosmopolitan versus local concerns. Rather, it embodied the attempts of Chicagoans to express and work out different concerns about how a new municipal government should be organized. One side in the conflict saw better government resulting from a small group having control of municipal affairs for a longer period of time. The other side viewed good urban government as coming from a situation that gave the majority of the voters a larger and more frequent voice in running the city. As the proponents of the latter view expressed it when they brought up the issue again toward the end of the convention, "the only excuse an alderman has for existing at all is because the people are too numerous to meet; therefore, it is his business to reflect the opinion, the desire, and the demand of his constituents." [14]

In and of itself, neither position described above is more valid than the other. To argue otherwise or to argue that one position is a more limited vision of municipal government is to miss the dynamics present in the urban reform movements of this period as urban residents struggled to redefine both their institutions and the nature of urban life in general. Keeping this sense of dynamics in mind while examining several of the important issues considered by the charter convention will make it possible to see both the ways in which Chicago's political culture helped shape differing ideas about urban reform within the city, and how for Chicago the convention and the subsequent ratification campaign provided a city-wide context for exploring these ideas and attempting to put them into practice.

Municipal Home Rule

Securing some home-rule powers for Chicago had been an avowed objective of the men who had begun the charter reform movement. Because any new charter would supersede the 1872 State Incorporation Act, many Chicagoans thought that it presented the perfect opportunity for redefining the relationship between

Chicago and the state government. However, it was quickly apparent to the delegates at the convention that there was no agreement about how to do this, neither among themselves, nor among the rest of the city.

Despite having declared only a few years earlier that one of its municipal reform priorities was to free Chicago from the dictates of the state legislature in local affairs, the Civic Federation had vigorously backed away from that stance by the time the convention opened. In fact, in 1902, the report prepared by the organization on the need for a new city charter neglected altogether to include home rule among its six propositions for a new scheme of local government.[15] At the same time, other groups within the city had begun to press for the inclusion of a strong home-rule provision in any new charter. The CFL, for instance, following the ratification of the enabling amendment, had passed, in early 1905, a resolution calling for a strong home-rule charter. The labor organization wanted a charter to grant the Chicago City Council complete control of the city's streets, public utilities, franchises, street railways, municipal services, and, in general, to remove all control of the state legislature over local government and business affairs; it was willing to concede the state control only in the areas of public safety, health, and the general commerce and communication needs of the state.[16]

When the matter of home rule arose at the convention, however, there was little discussion about theories of home rule. Instead, the delegates argued over the legal viability of any home-rule provision in the charter. On the one side, delegate Joseph O'Donnell pressed the case that legally Chicago was now free to write whatever home-rule measure it desired. He insisted that the terms of the enabling amendment "liberated us here in Chicago from the general laws in this state and said that what could only be done heretofore by general laws, now can be done by local and special laws peculiar to the City of Chicago." Delegate David Shanahan disputed this interpretation, arguing that in fact the amendment only allowed the legislature to pass special legislation for Chicago, a power it had lacked under the incorporation act, and did not give Chicago its own home-rule powers.[17] Neither position had been tested in court, but the sentiment of the convention overwhelmingly favored the conservative interpretation of the amendment, and, as a result, the delegates wrote a weak home-rule provision into the new charter, specifying that the city did not intend to assume any home-rule powers that would conflict with general state laws. Following the arguments of delegates Merriam and Fisher that courts throughout the country generally construed very strictly the powers conferred upon municipalities, the convention moved even further away from attempting to secure home rule by passing a provision acknowledging the superior legal position of the state in regard to all municipal affairs.[18]

Why, when the opportunity presented itself, did the convention shy away from even attempting to secure home rule? Since certain cities in the country had already obtained a measure of home rule stronger than that which the delegates were willing to settle for in Chicago, they could not have been certain that the courts would have rejected a home-rule charter. And, because the charter undoubtedly would have to be bargained out with the legislature, why not adopt the tactic of asking for more to begin with, so that certain points could be softened or conceded if necessary? Aside from arguing the legalities of the question, the convention as a whole was very silent on this issue, and an understanding of why they opposed more home rule can be reached only by understanding the relationship between this and other municipal issues.

Conceding the primacy of state laws gave the delegates an easy escape from some problems that they did not want to confront directly. The most troubling of these issues was that of liquor regulation. As discussed earlier, the prevailing sentiment in the city was strongly antiprohibition; that in the state was clearly the opposite. The prohibition forces were beginning to concentrate their full energies on Chicago, where a number of men involved in charter reform, though not favoring prohibition themselves, did not want to run afoul of groups such as the Law and Order League, Anti-Saloon League, and Hyde Park Protective Association, whose support they wanted on other reform issues. However, straddling the fence on this issue had become particularly difficult for them in the first years of the new century as the temperance forces intensified their efforts to compel the city and the state to regulate more stringently the sale of liquor in Chicago.

The convention delegates were caught between the prohibition forces on the one side and the United Societies for Local Self-Government on the other, each wanting the new charter to embody its position on liquor. The latter organization had petitioned the convention to vest the city council with complete home-rule powers to regulate liquor in the city, believing that if the decision on liquor were left to the people of Chicago they would decisively defeat prohibition.[19] For the opposition, delegate Frank Bennett had proposed a resolution that nothing in the charter give the council power to modify, impair, or conflict with the state laws regulating the sale of liquor. The Organization of Methodist Episcopal Preachers had communicated to the convention its congregations' support of Bennett's resolution and its desire that the charter "be proposed in such a form that they can give it their heartiest support, with the assurances that the moral interests of Chicago are safeguarded thereby."[20] Bombarded by both sides on this sticky issue, the convention delegates could avoid taking any stand at all on the issue of liquor regulation by bowing to the primacy of state laws and not providing a generous grant of home rule in the charter. Moreover, whenever they reached a similarly uncomfortable issue in the course of the convention, they adopted the same tactic, as will be explained later in this chapter.

Another explanation for why a stronger push was not made for home rule lies in the adage that the essence of home rule was really who ruled at home. The continuing control of the legislature over municipal affairs provided assurance that more radical elements within the city would never be able to organize and run the city in the ways they deemed best. Many businessmen and political conservatives still feared a radical takeover of Chicago. This fear was, in fact, being abetted at that time by the "radical" mayoral administration of Democrat Edward Dunne. Dunne's appointees to the board of education, especially Raymond Robins, a social worker, and Louis Post, who was committed to the single tax, had considerably shaken the business community's grip on the school system. Furthermore, just when businessmen were feeling secure that they had defeated municipal ownership of public utilities, Dunne switched sides and renewed his earlier pledge to reject new traction franchises in favor of immediate municipal ownership.[21] During the spring 1907 mayoral election campaign that coincided with the closing days of the convention, the Republican candidate Fred Busse was promoted as the man who could "settle for many years the question as to whether the long haired men and short haired women are going to rule and ruin this town." Following Busse's election, the *Tribune* raved about the intelligent decision finally made by Chicago, "the most radical city in the world."[22] Surely that description was a bit hyperbolic, but it indicated the fears lingering among certain segments of the population about the possibilities of a radical takeover of the government. Thus, there would be, for these men, a certain security in knowing that the rurally dominated state legislature would always be able to put a stop to the more radical trends within Chicago if the city did not have any strong home-rule powers.

It was for the same reason that the convention delegates shied away from establishing powers of referendum and initiative in the new charter. As broad home-rule powers would have given the city more say over its municipal affairs, the power to initiate legislation and ratify it by referendum vote would have given the citizens of Chicago a greater share and more direct control over the municipal government. In both 1902 and 1904, the voters had signified their desire for these political innovations in public-policy referenda,[23] and the issues were certain to rise at the convention, as indeed they did. Now the CFL led a fight to include the initiative and referendum in the charter, sending a letter to the convention demanding that the charter give both powers to the voters, with the signatures of 5 percent of the registered voters needed to enact either measure. According to the labor organization, only these powers would bring municipal democracy to Chicago and prevent the "vulgar aristocracy" from running things to suit itself.[24]

Many delegates expressed some sympathy for the principle

of more direct popular involvement in municipal government, but they were very cautious about putting the initiative and referendum into the charter itself. Delegates Snow and Eckhart said they would only agree to a conservative referendum measure, one that required the signatures of 25 percent of the voters. Such a percentage, they said, would "show that a very respectable minority of the people" supported the calling of a referendum. Twenty-five percent was a good deal higher than the 5 percent limit sought by the CFL. Charles Merriam supported a compromise measure of 15 percent and observed that if a question was important enough to secure fifty or sixty thousand votes (approximately 15 percent), it was unfair to require more, but the convention still balked at the lower figure.[25] In the end, the delegates first set a 20 percent figure on the calling of a referendum, then lowered that figure to 10 percent at the convention's last session. By then, they felt confident enough that other safeguards in the charter would protect them against too much popular democracy. They did, however, refuse altogether to provide powers to initiate legislation.[26]

Finally, and very importantly, the convention delegates could concede the issue of home rule to the state government because for many of these men, the conception of a well-run municipal government did not include extensive home-rule powers. What the majority of these men was most interested in was achieving fiscal and administrative reform, primarily by modifying the existing structure through some consolidation of overlapping governing authorities, and obtaining a little more fiscal flexibility than currently existed. This position came out very clearly in the convention discussions over fiscal reforms.

Municipal Revenues

No one in Chicago seriously questioned the need for reform of the city's revenue situation. What kind of reform was the critical question, and at the convention three proposals were considered. The first, made by James Linehan and Louis Post, proposed complete home rule for Chicago in determining its revenue system. Arguing that the enabling amendment allowed Chicago to assume full powers to assess, levy, and collect taxes for corporate purposes,[27] Linehan and Post urged the convention simply to vest in the city council full power to raise revenue for municipal purposes. Having already rejected the idea of giving home-rule legislative powers to the city, the delegates were not inclined to look favorably upon a proposal to do the same for taxing powers. This resolution was even more unappealing because it further recommended that, as a check against council abuse of such power, a mandatory popular referendum on revenue matters also be effected by the new charter.[28] Charles Merriam firmly rejected this proposal. It was essential, he said, to have "certain financial restrictions and limitations and safeguards upon the power of the city," along with fixed statuatory limits on bonded indebtedness and taxing rates. The delegates felt the same way, as they voted decisively against this proposal.[29]

Merriam himself, however, put forth another proposal that would have significantly altered the municipal revenue system. Something of an expert on this problem because of a massive study he had undertaken for the City Club of Chicago, Merriam stunned many of his fellow delegates by proposing that they create a city tax system to replace the county-wide system to which they were currently bound. His research had convinced him that Chicago would only be able to control its revenues if it had the power to determine its own property assessments and taxation—an impossibility under the prevailing laws, which gave this power to the Cook County Board of Assessors. If Chicago could raise its property valuation it would be able to borrow more money (municipal indebtedness being tied to property value), thereby ensuring adequate funds for municipal expenses, making the city primarily responsible and accountable to the citizens for its expenditures, and possibly even lowering the tax rate. To allay their suspicions about such a radical change, Merriam assured his fellow delegates that all other large cities in the country currently controlled their own tax assessment, collection, and distribution.[30] Linehan joined Merriam in his resolution. He asked "Shall ninety-two percent of the voting people do the assessing or shall eight percent?" But the convention backed away from this idea as resolutely as it had backed away from the first proposal.[31]

Instead of introducing radical change into the revenue system, the majority of delegates was satisfied that the consolidation scheme in the charter provided adequate means for raising more money. Under this scheme, as specified in the 1904 amendment, the city's bonding power would automatically increase to 5 percent of full property valuation and its tax levy to 5 percent of assessed valuation. The only thing necessary for the charter convention to do was to devise a new system for control and disbursement of revenues once they had been received by the city. Accordingly, the delegates wrote a provision giving the city council power to determine annually the respective amounts to be levied each for corporate, park, school, and library purposes from the 5 percent tax collected on assessed property valuation. Most of the delegates favored this system because, unlike the prevailing fixed-percentage system, it would give the city more flexibility to vary its expenditures yearly according to where the money was needed most. Some delegates did express doubts about leaving the annual levies unspecified. They were especially worried about chronic underfunding of the school system and proposed an amendment to set a minimum yearly amount to be appropriated for running the schools. This, too, was defeated; consolidation and flexible levies were the only significant changes the charter was to make in Chicago's revenue system.[32]

The Public Schools

Having rejected the idea of broad municipal home rule and radical proposals for altering the city's revenue structure, the convention turned its attention to another acrimonious issue: what to do about the public school system. Unlike the previous two issues, where debate could be terminated by pleading the impossibilities of the legal situation or where moderate men could be persuaded to reject anything sounding too radical, there was no easy retreat from arguments over the schools. Most people in the city had an opinion about the school system, especially since the appointment of Mayor Dunne's "radical" school board currently had the city in an uproar. Thus, the issue provoked a protracted debate within the convention, a debate that was fueled by the intensity of feeling among the delegates themselves and by the submission of several contrary petitions from citizens outside. It was over this issue of the public schools that the charter convention became a public forum for conflicting viewpoints. The arguments over schools illustrate clearly both the differing ideas that Chicagoans had begun to develop about urban government and the ways in which the citizens had come to think of the charter as the medium through which to reshape their city.

In early October of 1906, the Merchants' Club delivered a petition to the convention, asking that its committee on education be allowed to assist the convention's education committee in drafting charter provisions to reorganize Chicago's schools on a "rational and business-like basis."[33] The writing of a new charter gave the Merchants' Club the perfect opportunity to reform the school system in the ways that prominent men in the city had been advocating for some years. As much as a decade earlier, a *Tribune* editorial had advocated an appointive board composed of "men of integrity, . . . thorough-going, educated businessmen, of whom Chicago has a large supply." Not content just to promote businessmen for the board of education, the newspaper went on to say that these men "should be able to speak the English language correctly and should at least have been educated in this country. The Board of Education is no place for nobodies."[34] Because Chicago was a city of immigrants, such standards automatically would have ruled out many citizens, including some prominent figures in the city; the *Tribune*'s statement itself, moreover, implied that large numbers of the citizenry were "nobodies."

Offended by this type of rhetoric and alarmed by other developments within the charter convention, the CFL called a special meeting to protest a drift toward making the schools a preserve of businessmen. Board member Louis Post, one of Dunne's "radicals," spoke to the meeting, accusing the convention of being in league with businessmen to design an educational system "drawn up by a few members of the Merchants' Club in the back room of the Union League Club" to attempt "through the proposed charter to wrest the control of the public schools from the people."[35] Other Chicagoans also distrusted the motives of the Merchants' Club and other business organizations regarding the schools. In a letter she sent to Lincoln Steffens, Margaret Dreier Robins, a prominent figure in the Chicago Women's Trade Union League and wife of board-of-education member Raymond Robins, asked Steffens to come to Chicago to expose the plotting of business, "the privileged interests of the city," to take over the schools. "Mass meetings," she wrote Steffens, "are called by these reverend gentlemen 'to consider the crisis in the public schools', and a petition has been signed by Mr. Gustavus Swift, packer, and others to be sent to the Charter Convention 'to curb the power of the School Board.' The Merchants' Club is preparing a 'ripper' bill to present to the next legislature to legislate the present school Board out of existence."[36] At the same time, the City Club of Chicago was commissioning its own Committee on Public Education with the task of seeking remedies to the school crisis that would "secure a more effective business administration and an education . . . more in accordance with the demands of modern society and business conditions."[37] Rounding out the business community's assault on the schools, the Commercial Club was promoting the institution of a dual school system of regular schools and industrial training schools.[38]

The CFL fired off a counterpetition to the convention, demanding that the charter provide for electing school-board members, paying them an adequate salary, and vesting full control of the public schools in the board and not in the superintendent. In its petition, the CFL also reminded the delegates that the voters had recently approved a public-policy measure to change the board of education from an appointive to an elective body. The CFL warned the delegates that its members would accept nothing short of these demands, and it promised that they would "resist by every honorable means any attempt of any and all interests and influences to take away the control of the Chicago school system from the people of Chicago."[39]

Following up on the CFL's recommendations on schools, three proposals were put before the convention that had as their objective the broadening, rather than the narrowing, of control of the schools. First, Louis Post and Raymond Robins proposed an elected school board to replace the current method of mayoral selection and thereby put the board in closer touch with the people as a whole, rather than the politicians or those people who had influence with the politicians at the moment of selection. When this resolution failed by a vote of thirty-nine to eleven,[40] James Linehan introduced a measure to pay salaries of $2500 to the people serving on the board of education. Delegate B. A. Eckhart, speaking in favor of maintaining an unpaid board, immediately objected that pay for board members would draw the wrong kind of people into service on the board. "I am of the opinion too that you will get a much abler class of men and more competent men if you rely upon their willingness to serve this community." James Linehan retorted that "the great civic pride which brings a millionaire who has no children . . . into the mayor's office every year endeavoring to get an appointment on the school board is not any more worthy of recognition than the pride of the workmen, who supply all the children and all the money for the maintenance of the public institutions of this city."[41] Those were the people least able to afford to serve on an unpaid board. But by refusing to consider any means that would have made it possible to surmount this obstacle, the convention delegates were saying quite clearly that they wanted to keep a tight restriction on the people serving on this body. Robins pointed out, in support of Linehan's proposal, that paid school board members would automatically become more accountable to the citizens because their tax monies paid the salaries. Few men at the convention were interested in this type of broad accountability or in making it easier for more people to serve on the school board. They rejected a paid school board.[42]

In one last attempt to change the direction into which the charter provisions on schools were headed, Post offered two measures that would have removed control over several important features of the system from the office of the superintendent. First, he proposed to transfer to the board the powers to introduce textbooks and to appoint, promote, and transfer teachers and principals. When the delegates rejected this proposal,[43] he sought to enhance the position of teachers, the "backbone of the system." The charter, he proposed, should give teachers direct access to the board with their suggestions on education and guarantee that their salaries would never be reduced during their tenure in the system. He pointed out that this last guarantee would only be fair since it was being extended in the new charter to the superintendent and the business manager of the school system. The convention rejected this measure as swiftly as it had rejected Post's previous proposals.[44]

There was certainly an element of class awareness in this issue—it was the children of the working class, after all, who principally attended the public schools. But what is often overlooked in assessing an issue such as public school reform, is what people were doing with this awareness. Post and Linehan were not rejecting reform; rather, they were rejecting a particular method of reform and its underlying assumptions and aims, and they were proposing alternatives. There also can be no denying the importance of public education in shaping the opportunities available to future generations of urban residents. In the early twentieth century in Chicago, both sides in the conflict were attempting to restructure an educational system for the future. They had assessed the existing system, found it wanting, and fought to establish new goals and methods for running an urban school system. One side in the conflict over school reform made businesslike efficiency and fiscal control of the schools its priority. The other side wanted a broader representation throughout the city on the policies and educational priorities of the system. Both sides in the contest knew that if an appointed superintendent and board of education with an ear to the business community were to run the schools, far different decisions were likely to result than from an elected board that hired the superintendent and was responsible to the voters.

Raymond Robins found it "a curious idea . . . voiced quite generally in this convention that seems to put the business efficiency of the school board as its supreme function."[45] But historians have all too frequently accepted uncritically the rhetoric of those urban residents who spoke glowingly about the benefits that "progressive" fiscal expertise and businesslike efficiency in the schools would bring to the city. Adopting the reformers' viewpoint, they automatically categorized those who proposed the reforms as progressives and those who opposed them as conservatives, even when the evidence pointed to something else at work. In assessing school reform in Atlanta, where there was strong public opposition to "reform" policies, one recent study established such a dichotomy between "progressives," who wanted certain reforms, and "conservatives," who did not. At the same time, the study acknowledged that business efficiency had brought teachers double shifts and mandatory teaching in summer schools with no increase in pay; that reformers had attempted to "provide differentiated curricula for students of different social classes"; and that in their emphasis on business efficiency, the reformers "made it clear that school officials would define these [citizens'] needs; that students would be trained in public schools for jobs in private business; and that reform would be accomplished with public funds doled out in a penurious manner by cost-conscious officials."[46] In the face of such evidence, there is ample reason why a significant portion of Atlanta's residents would have resisted these so-called reforms, and it had little to do with them being progressives or conservatives.

Because they resisted the reform proposals presented by people who identified themselves as "progressive" does not ipso facto make their opponents conservatives. In Chicago, Raymond Robins, Margaret Dreier Robins, Louis Post, the CFL, and the Chicago Federation of Teachers proposed an entirely different scheme of school reform. Under their proposal, the school system would have become more democratic, more subject to the influence of the broader community, rather than having its influence narrowed even further, and it would have made the teachers more, rather than less, involved in curriculum planning and the determination of school policies. For Post, it was the teachers who should have been considered the "experts" in education, not businessmen.[47] This was not a stand to excite the hearts of businessmen or "experts" in fiscal affairs. The Chicago Federation of Teachers was threatening already to become a major force in the school system, and if there was one thing the business "experts" did not want, it was a stronger teachers union. For more than a decade, the CFT had been a thorn in the side of businessmen and the school superintendent. Organized by the female elementary school teachers in 1897 to fight an attempt to rescind their newly won pension fund, the teachers' union had subsequently involved itself in other municipal affairs, especially anything regarding schools.[48] That there was also an element of sex discrimination in the convention's attempt to keep teachers out of school affairs cannot be denied. Margaret Haley, head of the CFT, was constantly belittled in the public press—the *Tribune* depicted her as one of the "short-haired women" running the radical administration of Edward Dunne. At the convention itself, Post accused his fellow delegates of having among their reasons for rejecting an elected school board the fact that women would be able to vote for school board members according to a state law of 1891.[49]

Both sides involved in the charter conflict over education policies and priorities were trying to come to grips with the problems of running a massive urban school system in a society that preached opportunity of education for all its children. This concept needs to be weighed when assessing proposals for educational reform in early-twentieth-century American cities. There existed no clear-cut standard against which to measure these proposals, because the concept of universal public education was still a recent idea. Arguments over school reform in Chicago's charter movement were part of working out how to provide such education, how to decide who would control the schools, and how to run the schools. Chicagoans held different ideas about their city's system of public education, but different does not automatically imply better or worse.

Home Rule Again: Suffrage, Liquor, Public Utilities

The delegates' resolve to avoid placing in the charter any specific home-rule provisions that might open up control of municipal affairs to a broader segment of the citizenry did not weaken as they considered three more controversial issues. The week following Christmas 1906, they had to tackle two of these issues, which they had put off until most other provisions of the charter had been agreed upon.

One of these issues was whether to grant municipal suffrage to women. As noted in chapter 1, many women in the city had grown increasingly concerned about and involved in muni-

cipal affairs over the past decade. When it was decided to write a
new charter, these women, whose numbers were drawn from
across the spectrum of social and economic classes, saw an opportunity to secure the vote. The Women's Trade Union League
requested the CFL to work to secure the municipal vote for
women in the charter; the Chicago Woman's Club sent its members a letter informing them of the possibility of securing the
franchise through the new charter and urged them to do whatever they could to help accomplish it.[50] From Hull-House, Jane
Addams headed a federation of one hundred women's organizations working for this same goal. The variety of women seeking
the vote and their reasons impressed her. "We were joined," she
wrote, "by organizations of working women who had keenly felt
the need of the municipal franchise in order to secure for their
workshops the most rudimentary sanitation . . . by federations
of mothers' meetings, who were interested in clean milk and the
extension of kindergartens . . . by property-owning women, who
had been powerless to protest against unjust taxation; by organizations of professional women, of university students, and of
collegiate alumnae; by women's clubs interested in municipal
reforms."[51] Addams' experience with the investigations of her
Hull-House Women's Club into the garbage, street cleaning, and
other sanitation problems in their neighborhood had persuaded
her that these were city-wide problems that could not be attacked piecemeal or through voluntary means and that women
now needed the political power of the vote behind their efforts.
As she saw it, when even the immigrant women of her impover-
ished neighborhood were telling her that they wanted the right
to vote, women all across the city had developed a sense of "public concern" that now had to be granted the means of political
expression.[52]

Not all women agreed, of course, and the Illinois Association Opposed to the Extension of Suffrage to Women petitioned
the convention not to grant municipal suffrage.[53] To counter this
petition, the Illinois Equal Suffrage Association asked Raymond
Robins to lead the fight for suffrage in the convention, and
women representing both sides of the question appeared before
the convention committee on elections.[54] When the committee

voted five to four against recommending woman suffrage in the new charter, Louis Post asked that women be allowed to address directly the whole convention, since they lacked direct representation in that body for presenting their case. Delegate B. A. Eckhart spoke against extending this privilege to women, protesting that "it would be a mistake to open this convention to everyone who desires to be heard upon any subject." There was no way the majority of delegates was going to support turning the convention into a popular assembly, and they quickly quashed this idea.[55]

Nonetheless, those men who supported municipal suffrage for women did raise the issue before the convention. Delegate White argued eloquently that women should be able to vote because they were taxpayers, had vital interests in urban affairs, could not be assumed to agree with their husbands—could not, in fact, be assumed to have husbands—and were already quite active in municipal affairs. Not extending them the vote, he said, would be "an injustice to the working women of Chicago, it is wrong and it is absolutely unAmerican." Opponents of this measure spoke just as vigorously against it, with sexism and the desire to avoid extending the vote into the wrong areas both playing equal roles. Typical of their reasoning were the pleas of delegates against "dragging women down from the pedestal to mix in ward politics" and against polluting "her tenderness, . . . those feminine qualities which particularly appeal to men," by allowing women to wallow in the muck of politics.[56]

The other part of the argument against suffrage cut more to the heart of the matter as far as many of the delegates were concerned. They warned that suffrage would give the wrong class of women a vote in municipal affairs, and "that the influence of the ladies that we seek to obtain will not be obtained."[57] As they had before in other matters that threatened to disrupt the balance of political power in the city, the delegates again took refuge in deferring to the preeminent position of the state legislature, maintaining that giving women suffrage in the new charter was not among the grants of power bestowed upon the city in the 1904 enabling amendment. The prevailing sentiment of the convention remained against placing in the new charter any provisions that conferred home-rule power on Chicago, and a request for women suffrage fell within those bounds. Thus, the delegates refused to place municipal suffrage for women in the new charter.[58]

However, the issue was not so easily resolved. In attempting to surmount the objections that the charter could not legally confer this right upon women, the Equal Suffrage Association adopted a different tactic. It requested several delegates to ask the convention instead to submit to the legislature, along with the charter, a separate bill for female municipal suffrage in Chicago. If the legislature ratified this bill, it, along with the charter, would be returned to the Chicago voters for ratification. The belief of the Equal Suffrage Association was that enough people in Chicago supported the idea that now that the municipal government was being reformed, this reform too should be introduced in the city. The delegates, however, refused to consider women suffrage even in this manner.[59]

If the question of municipal suffrage for women was a ticklish one for the delegates to handle, the problem of municipal regulation of liquor was downright unpleasant and an issue that they put off for as long as they could. Ultimately, however, as there was no escaping it, on December 27, 1906, the convention considered the various petitions that had been placed before it regarding this issue.

Since its founding convention the previous May, the United Societies for Local Self-Government had led a drive to place home-rule power on liquor regulation into the charter. At that convention, the United Societies had argued that it saw liquor regulation as a question of home rule and that the charter was the perfect instrument for severing the state legislature's control both over liquor regulation and municipal affairs in general. The United Societies had ended its convention by issuing a declaration of its principles and purposes, emphasizing its position "that in a democratic republic the laws should conform to the views and wishes of the broad citizenry as well as the actual existing social conditions. Obsolete and neglected restrictive laws . . . stand in contradiction to popular government and should either be reformed or abolished." The declaration also stated the belief of the United Societies that the prevailing differences between Chicago, or any urban community, and a highly rural state such as Illinois necessitated that cities have home-rule power to determine how they were going to regulate themselves in all manner of purely municipal affairs.[60]

To argue, as some studies have, that in Chicago and elsewhere the conflict over liquor regulation was a cultural conflict between old-stock Protestants and new-stock, primarily Catholic immigrants in which the latter group was seeking freedom from government on issues of "right behavior" misses the opportunity to examine the urban dynamic taking place in late-nineteenth- and early-twentieth-century cities.[61] The writing of a new municipal charter for Chicago gave everyone in the city, including its ethnic population, a chance to consider what kind of city they wanted to live in and what kind of urban government they wanted to structure in order to attain that kind of urban life. As will become more apparent in the chapter on the ratification campaign, liquor regulation was only one aspect of the United Societies' dealings on the charter. When everything is taken into account, it is possible to see the ways in which the United Societies' "personal liberty" rhetoric was more of a rhetorical device than a cultural stand.

The link that the United Societies made between specific home rule on liquor regulation and general home-rule powers for the city is evidence for this broader vision. In early December 1906, the organization requested the delegates to include a provision in the charter that specifically vested the city council with sole power to regulate Sunday closings and the sale of liquor at social gatherings and entertainments, saying that "we believe that we reflect the sentiment of four-fifths of the voters of our city on this subject. . . . We demand home rule on this question and believe the city council can be trusted to so regulate both matters as to satisfy the true religious sentiments and wants of the large majority of our citizens."[62] When the convention first deferred the question of liquor regulation until some future session and then refused to write a strong home-rule charter, the United Societies grew more fearful that prohibition was virtually certain under the new charter as it was taking shape. The organization petitioned the delegates anew, asking them both to reconsider their stand on liquor regulation and to provide a strong home-rule provision giving the city council "all powers of local legislation which may under the constitution be vested in a municipality."[63]

The United Societies believed that there was a grave danger of prohibition in Chicago if the charter failed either to be a strong home-rule charter or to include a specific provision about liquor regulation. Legally, when a new charter was ratified, the city might well find itself bound by any general state laws that were not specifically nullified by this new charter. Although this legal position was untested in the courts, there was a sound basis for this fear. A new charter would supersede the 1872 State Incorporation Act, and it was this act that, up to this point, had provided Chicago with a legal loophole for regulating liquor. Thus, despite increasing pressure from antiliquor forces, Chicago had so far avoided having to enforce the general state laws still on the books that mandated Sunday closings of saloons.[64] Moreover, without home-rule power on liquor regulation in the new charter, Chicago would surely find itself subject to future state laws regarding liquor.

Throughout December, the United Societies gathered support for its position. The CFL leadership gave ready support to the claims that the majority of Chicagoans did not want Sunday closings. Sunday, the CFL pointed out, was the only day on which workers could "relax, enjoy themselves, and recover from their arduous weekly labors." They urged all workers to join with the United Societies' efforts to ensure that saloons and other places of entertainment would not be closed to them on their one day off work.[65] More and more ethnic organizations joined the United Societies and pledged to support the home-rule petitions set before the convention.[66]

The temperance forces in Chicago urged the delegates to keep any home rule on liquor out of the charter because they agreed with both the United Societies' assessment of popular sentiment on this issue and the likelihood that without home rule in the charter the city would be subject to all general state laws. In a letter to Raymond Robins, Robert McCurdy, a spokesman for the Law and Order League, stressed that Chicago needed the protection of state laws to avoid being handed over to the forces of vice and corruption. Any kind of home-rule provisions, but most especially on liquor regulation, McCurdy warned Robins, would enable Chicago to "license prostitution and race track gambling, do away with the provisions of the Sunday closing law and to undoubtedly exempt itself from numerous other provisions of the Criminal Code." McCurdy also had future legislation in mind when he wrote this letter to Robins. He was confident that the next session of the legislature would pass a new local option law making it easier to implement prohibition districts in the city.[67]

That the members of the Law and Order League in Chicago saw themselves as acting in tandem with state-wide prohibition forces to circumvent the overwhelmingly negative sentiment in the city toward prohibition is certain. "I hope that you will believe with me," continued McCurdy in his letter to Robins, "that on these questions it is better to have the more conservative and more American sentiment of the country to help us out rather than to leave the whole matter to the population of Chicago at this time. . . . [W]hen our foreign increment has been digested, it might be different."[68] Small wonder that the United Societies felt that the attempt to keep home rule on liquor out of the charter was the work of forces outside of the city, who were trying to tell the people of Chicago how they could live, and the organization was quick to accuse those convention delegates leading the fight against a provision for home rule on liquor of being in collusion with these state-wide forces.[69] From its perspective, the United Societies was confronting a clearly defined situation: the majority of the city did not favor prohibition; but a minority, in league with those rural state-wide forces who for decades had been expressing through statement and laws their loathing for Chicago, were attempting to force their will on the rest of the citizenry.

For the United Societies, the time to put a stop to state interference in liquor and municipal affairs in general had arrived. The organization warned Chicagoans that failure to include home-rule provisions in the charter might not just affect the sale of liquor; ultimately the situation could turn against them in other ways. For instance, the same state laws that mandated Sunday closings could be used to ban theaters, the running of streetcars, the publishing and selling of newspapers—any activity that might be construed as disturbing the peace on Sunday. All of these activities, the United Societies pointed out, along with other forms of Sunday entertainments, had become vital parts of the cosmopolitan urban life of Chicago. To ban any of them would greatly alter the nature of that life. The charter, the United Societies argued, was the opportunity for Chicagoans to try to seize control of the mechanisms of their government and shape them to assure that, from this time onward, they would decide for themselves how they were going to order life in their city, no longer to be dictated to by forces outside on issues that concerned only those who lived within.[70]

The city's ethnic population, or working class, did not stand entirely alone in this. It found support at the convention, for instance, from delegate Alexander Revell, a wealthy Republican furniture manufacturer. Revell supported the idea that the charter should contain a provision giving the city home-rule powers to regulate liquor, for "then the people of Chicago can decide whether they want Sunday saloons or not. And it is the people's right, in a land of popular government to have such laws as they desire." A few other delegates agreed that this was squarely an issue of home rule, but the convention as a whole simply did not want to get caught between the opposing forces on this issue, and it refused to place such a provision in the charter. The delegates did, however, readily agree to write a separate bill on liquor regulation for Chicago and to submit it to the legislature along with the charter.[71]

Thus, for the question of liquor regulation, the delegates were willing to take the extra step that they had refused to countenance for women suffrage. Why was this the case? Creating a mass of new and potentially uncontrollable voters evidently seemed much more dangerous to the convention than the possibility of keeping saloons open on Sundays. In fact, for some delegates, this compromise seemed a way to "have their cake and eat it too." Women suffrage would have reordered the way the whole city functioned, and it was not clear, as several of the delegates had earlier pointed out, that they could predict or control the outcome of this reform. But a separate bill on liquor regulation posed no such threat. Certain delegates, among them some who later in February would staunchly oppose a separate bill on women suffrage, saw liquor regulation as a local matter rather than one that would affect municipal government as a whole. "This is distinctly and essentially [a local issue]," declared delegate Rosenthal, "upon which the neighborhood ought to dictate what should be done in a particular locality, even in the City of Chicago." For Rosenthal, a separate bill, that might or might not pass the legislature, was first of all an expedient: it would allow the convention to negotiate safe passage between two opposing camps and keep this volatile issue out of the charter itself. Moreover, Rosenthal believed that when the state legislature did ratify a new local option bill it would facilitate the creation of more prohibition districts in the city if the new charter contained home-rule powers on liquor.[72]

Although in the end the convention delegates could afford to be quasi-benevolent on the issue of municipal regulation of liquor, they stood more firmly opposed to one final home-rule issue, that of municipal ownership of public utilities. Like women suffrage, they saw municipal ownership as an innovation that would clearly affect the running of the city as a whole in ways that many of the delegates had been opposing for the past few years.[73] Furthermore, municipal ownership was an avowed goal of the CFL and of "radical" reform groups in the city. There was simply no doubt that these businessmen delegates were not going to place a provision in the new charter mandating immediate municipal ownership. Consequently, no such provision ever even came to a vote. The convention did listen, however, to the "sensible" voice of delegate Walter Fisher, who was also the city's official consultant on this issue. Fisher's position was that the city had to adopt adequate and effective public control and regulation of utilities, both to eliminate existing franchise abuses and to prevent future abuses, and at the same time to satisfy enough of the prevailing public outrage against these abuses to undercut those people agitating for immediate municipal ownership.[74] Because most representatives at the convention, as well as most people in the city, agreed with Fisher that some type of franchise reform was absolutely necessary, the delegates followed his recommendations and placed in the new charter certain provisions designed to safeguard the city's ability to regulate public utilities. These provisions included one that extended to all public utilities the municipal privileges granted in the recent state law on traction—the Mueller Law. This was the law that conferred upon Illinois cities the power to build or buy and operate streetcar lines under certain conditions. It cost the delegates nothing to include this provision in the new charter, for they believed it highly unlikely that the advocates of immediate municipal ownership would ever succeed in their campaign under its provisions. The delegates also strengthened in the charter the city's power to regulate rates charged by utilities and forbade the city council ever to limit or grant away this latter right.[75] These provisions were easy for the delegates to grant because they satisfied the need for public utility reforms without having to resort to municipal ownership. Municipal ownership would have undercut businessmen to begin with, but even worse in the view of most delegates was that if the city actually operated utilities, there would be the danger of too much popular control over the building and running of public utilities should the wrong people gain control of the municipal government.

After these provisions had been approved by the convention, a few delegates presented another motion regarding public utilities. They asked that a provision be included in the charter to repeal the rights of frontage consents. Under existing municipal law, property owners had the right to veto the placement of public utilities on streets fronting their property. With this proposed measure, the city would be unimpeded in deciding the best places to locate new public utilities. This proposal, when viewed in tandem with another proposal on the enforcement of municipal tenement ordinances discussed next, presents an opportunity to reconsider a cardinal thesis of urban progressive reform—that of the cosmopolitan versus local perspective of "reformers" and their opponents. Despite the rhetoric advanced by many of the men most actively involved in charter reform in Chicago that they were the urban residents who had the good of the entire city in mind, few of these delegates were willing to place public good over private profit when it might adversely affect them personally. Speaking against repeal of frontage consents, delegate B. W. Snow said, "Now it is all very well to say that the general good requires the building of this line or that line, but I maintain that the right of the property owner himself should be considered."[76] A majority of the delegates readily agreed with this position. They were property owners themselves, and the motion was decisively beaten back.

Yet, on another issue that might easily be construed as one in which the rights of property owners were similarly at stake, the delegates did not necessarily vote in a similar fashion. The question this time was whether to strike from the charter a previously passed provision that gave the city council power to enforce tenement ordinances, if necessary by making repairs and passing the costs on to those owners who had refused to keep their property in compliance with the building codes. Delegate Frank Shepard argued in favor of striking this clause, saying that "it would always run against the property owner's wishes." But only five of the twenty delegates voting on both issues cast votes that could be attributed to protecting the rights of private property. Eight of the twenty voted not to repeal the right to frontage consents, while also voting to give the council the right to override the rights of property owners in enforcing tenement ordinances.[77] The votes cast on these two issues show that these delegates did not follow a consistent line of voting, either to preserve property rights or to put the common good ahead of private ownership. The personal welfare of these "reformers" sometimes took precedence over their concern for the municipal welfare. On the issue of giving the city the right to decide where to place public utilities, surely a crucial question for developing the city as a whole, many property-owning delegates refused to surrender to the common good. On the issue of tenement ordinances, most of the delegates readily agreed to put the needs of the city before those of private owners. Only if a vision of the city as a whole is defined as whatever these men decided it should be can one persist, with evidence like this, to credit the charter reformers with a true cosmopolitan vision. It would be better to say that they, like the rest of the people who were and would be involved in the charter campaign, were all working to redefine a vision of the city.

One final measure regarding municipal ownership needs to be considered, and on this one, the minority voice on franchise reform prevailed. At the convention's last session, Louis Post moved that the charter substitute a simple majority vote for a previously passed provision that a three-fifths majority of a popular vote was necessary to permit municipal operation of public utilities. He bolstered his case by pointing out that, according to other terms already placed in the charter, the city could acquire utilities with only a majority vote. Why, he asked, should the majority of the people not also be allowed to decide if the city should operate these utilities? Post's opponents hauled out their usual arguments against too much popular say in municipal affairs: Joseph Badenoch protested "that there is a large percentage of the unthinking part of the population that would always be ready to vote on anything that would change the existing conditions"; and Frank Bennett declared himself not one of those who believe that "the people themselves need no restraint."[78]

The delegates, nevertheless, ratified Post's proposal to loosen the strictures on popular votes over municipal operation of public utilities, but they did so without discussing this proposition to an extent that would allow ready inference about what these men were thinking. Their willingness to let this pass, therefore, must be seen in the context of what they had already accomplished in the charter to safeguard against too much popular voice in the municipal government. They had rejected a broad home-rule provision, had refused to create a new mass of voters by enfranchising women, and had sought to undercut the position of the radical proponents of municipal ownership by giving enough guarantees of moderate franchise reform in the charter without handing over too much control of the situation to the voters. Furthermore, in considering the issue of popular referendum, they had rejected a motion to allow the city council to submit any franchise grant to a referendum vote before it could be enacted. Delegate Revell had spoken against this idea, warning that it might imperil "good" franchises because a lot of people in the city were willing to vote against granting any franchises whatsoever. Delegate Hill had supported Revell's position, but was less tactful than Revell and put it in terms sure to antagonize many Chicago voters. He warned against giving the referendum on franchises because Chicago had a lot of foreign voters voting on questions which they did not understand. "They are voters before they understand our language; they are voters before their theory of government which they bring over with them is eliminated."[79]

The convention delegates had also more tightly secured their own position on public utilities by, at their final session, rejecting another motion by Post, this one to amend the clause already in the charter giving the city council a sixty-day option period in which to submit for referendum any franchise grant that would exceed five years' duration. Post wanted the charter to mandate a required referendum on such matters, arguing that "because this is public property the people should have a say in its distribution." Following Charles Merriam's objection that such a required referendum clause would lead to too many votes on anything perceived as a grant to a utility, the convention refused to ratify Post's motion.[80] Thus, while Post had achieved a small victory by reducing from three-fifths to a simple majority the popular margin needed to empower the city to operate public utilities, it was a small token. The majority of the delegates had, in other provisions, guaranteed a charter that would almost certainly assure that such radical innovations as municipal ownership and operation of public utilities would never occur. What the convention had achieved on this issue was far less radical or innovative than what other Chicagoans wanted, but the significance of this cannot be understood outside of the context of the whole charter movement. Ideas about franchise reform that may seem "progressive" in their content and have been judged so by other historians, were, in the context of other ideas and proposals in the city, actually conservative.

At the convention's final session, the vast majority of the delegates indicated that they were pleased with the charter which they had drafted. As well they should have been, because the charter embodied much of what they had set out to accomplish; with consolidation of overlapping governing authorities, revenue reform, an emphasis on business efficiency in the schools, no municipal ownership, and no extensive home-rule powers given either to the government itself or to the people, the charter would restructure the municipal government almost exactly as the Civic Federation had desired. At the end of the convention, the delegates were still unable to accept that there could be legitimate opposition to their charter. Milton Foreman, who had chaired the convention, in his closing statements heaped lavish praise upon the convention and its charter. "An inspection of the membership will disclose the fact that they represent every walk and condition and poll of thought in life," declared Foreman, adding that they were men who wrote "a charter not for their own purposes, not for their own use, not for their own benefit, but for the benefit of all the people of all the city for all time."[81] This was justified from his point of view, since it was his plan that had constituted the convention. Charles Merriam tempered this grandiose statement some by suggesting that opposition might indeed exist, but that now was the time for all reasonable men to compromise. "[Mr. Cole and I] agreed," he said, "to pledge ourselves, if the other gentlemen would do likewise, to accept this charter from this convention. I do not see how a man can act on principle and do otherwise."[82]

Louis Post, however, believed he could, and should, do otherwise. In his final speech before the convention he touched upon several of the issues that continued to rankle him and many other people in the city. Rejecting Merriam's assumptions, he told the delegates assembled for the last time, "I did not come into this convention with any determination to be absolutely governed by its decisions. If it had been a representative convention, elected by the people . . . then I should have considered that whatever conclusions that convention came to, I should fall in with the rest of the members. I did come, however . . . with the full determination, that if the members, even though appointed instead of elected, should formulate a home rule charter, a fair and good charter, that even if I did not like it in many respects, I would support it."[83] Alas, it was definitely not a home-rule charter, nor did Post believe it fair or agree with Foreman's assessment that it was a charter designed to benefit all the people of all the city. He refused to vote his acceptance of it.

Aside from Louis Post's opposition, which could have easily been predicted, one other event pricked the euphoric balloon of the delegates at their last session. Several of the delegates who were also state legislators refused to give their unqualified support to the charter, with the most ominous reasoning coming from one of these men who declared "that if the country members of the Legislature were able to prevail upon my judgment, that some of the Provisions of the Charter . . . were erroneous, founded upon wrong principles, then I would vote in favor of change."[84] His statement could not help but refocus attention for the charter campaign on the animosity between city and state and elevate the fears of many Chicagoans that unless they gained real home-rule powers—powers that they did not believe they would be granted with the present charter—they would always be at the mercy of a hostile state legislature. Between the objections of Post and those of the state legislators, an ominous note had sounded for the charter's future, but few men at the convention's closing session heard it. They packed up their papers, adjourned the convention, and set their minds to the task of getting the charter through the legislature unscathed.

FOUR

THE CHARTER AND THE POLITICIANS

*The Mayoral Election of 1907 and the Charter
in the State Legislature*

The charter convention had barely adjourned when political events in Chicago and Springfield sparked furious disagreements among Chicagoans that would intrude upon the optimistic outlook the charter's supporters held for its ratification. First, the 1907 mayoral campaign—a campaign noteworthy for its mudslinging nastiness—swung into high gear in early March. Simultaneously, the charter was sent to the state legislature for approval. And soon after these two events, the storm brewing over the board of education finally broke.

Looking back on those few months in 1907, it is possible to see that by the time the new mayor had finished his first two months in office and the legislature had ratified an amended version of the charter, the charter was virtually doomed for defeat. The municipal issues and the arguments over them that were sounded during the mayoral campaign, for instance, played into the political tensions within the city, helping split it into openly hostile political camps out of which few Chicagoans ventured during the later charter ratification campaign. The changes made to the charter by the legislators and the cavalier attitude with which certain charter supporters accepted these changes gave further evidence to many people in Chicago that the charter as written was unacceptable and designed for the benefit of a few, and this hardened their resolve to defeat it at the ballot box. The furor over appointments and dismissals of school board members further polarized the city into opposing political camps. When the fate of the reform charter is viewed in the context of these events surrounding it, the very tight connections between the charter's fate, Chicago's political culture, and different ideas about good municipal reform become more readily understandable.

The Mayoral Election of 1907

In 1907, the Republican party thought it stood a good chance of winning the mayoral race. The incumbent mayor, Edward Dunne, had alienated too many Chicago voters, either by being too wishy-washy or too radical on some important municipal issues. Moreover, the various factions of the Democratic party were not firmly behind Dunne and this intraparty feuding fueled the Republican hopes of regaining the office it had not controlled in a decade. For the Republicans, this mayoral contest was especially important because the winner would serve the first four-year term in that office; and if the new charter, which they were supporting, were ratified, the reorganization of municipal government would take place under whomever was in office. The party leaders, therefore, selected a candidate who they believed would enhance the chances of victory.

Their nominee was Fred A. Busse. Although leader of the north-side faction of the Republican party,[1] Busse was a political figure of comparatively minor stature, who was currently postmaster of Chicago and previously had served relatively inconspicuously in the state legislature. From the Republican perspective, Busse had two attractive qualities. First of all, he was so uncontroversial that no one in the party could say much against him. This was particularly important because the party wanted to exploit its opponent's weakness and present a united front to the voters. Second, Busse was German and a staunch supporter of the new charter. Of all the party's potential mayoral candidates, he was the man who could talk to the city's ethnic groups and help allay their fears that the new charter would bring prohibition to the city.

Just as the campaign was getting underway, Busse was injured in a train accident. He spent the remainder of the campaign in bed, and Chicago witnessed a mayoral race in which the Republican candidate gave no speeches and made no public appearances. But this was not an unfortunate turn of events for the candidate himself or for his party. According to one contemporary observer, the accident "relieved [Busse] from the necessity of a speechmaking campaign, which would not have been at all to his liking. He rarely talks in public."[2] The party coped easily with this situation, assuming complete control of the campaign and, by all accounts, turning it into one of the more scurrilous of Chicago mayoral races.[3]

The two most rancorous issues raised during the campaign— those that would haunt the charter campaign soon to follow— were traction reform and public school reform. In his mayoral campaign of 1905, Edward Dunne had promised to implement municipal ownership of street railways if elected. Soon after taking office, however, he had appointed Walter Fisher as his official traction adviser. Fisher, as he had shown at the convention, was committed to moderate franchise reform. Dunne agreed to follow Fisher's advice that the city not take over the existing traction franchises that had recently expired, but rather that the city renegotiate these franchises to receive better terms for the city. Yet shortly after Fisher had accomplished this task and presented new tractions agreements to the city council for approval, Dunne repudiated Fisher and the agreements. Labeling them insufficiently protective of the rights of the people who had to depend on public transit and not remunerative enough for the city, the mayor vetoed the agreements after they had passed the city council and renewed his earlier call for immediate municipal ownership.

The Republican party moved quickly to take advantage of Dunne's about-face, portraying him as indecisive and untrustworthy and calling both of his objections to the new traction

agreements unacceptable. To the party and much of its membership, the traction problem was not to be decided by the people,
but was a business matter to be settled by businessmen sitting
down together and hammering out the best deal for all concerned—that is, for all the businessmen concerned. State Attorney General William H. Stead sounded this theme at a Busse
rally when he declared that "the one thing needed in the present
[traction] crisis is plain, everyday common sense and business
judgment."[4] Because the main objective of many businessmen
was to secure a traction system that better served business, even
the compensation to the city negotiated in traction franchises
mattered far less than obtaining new franchises that promised
to provide the kind of transit system that business desired, running over the routes that it declared the most desireable. Republican Alderman Milton Foreman, who had chaired the charter
convention, dismissed opposing arguments that the renegotiated
franchises did not bring in sufficient revenue to the municipal
government, saying "what do we care whether the city makes $1
or $1 million out of the deal? The thing we are vitally interested
in is keeping a straight spine by getting a seat." And a Chicago
banker joined this chorus declaring that "the building up of a
new street car system is absolutely indispensable to the business life of the city. It would pay the people of Chicago to spend
almost any amount of money and upon almost any terms to
create an adequate transportation system for themselves in the
shortest possible time."[5]

Dunne and many of his supporters could not have disagreed
more completely with this assessment of the issue. Not only did
they object to the premise that the first purpose of public transit
was to serve business, they stood ideologically opposed to the
continuation of the franchise system. Municipal ownership for
them was not just a way of operating a mass transit system: it
contained the possibility that the people themselves, not just
businessmen, would have a significant voice in the crucial decisions to be made about the transit system—where and when, for
instance, traction lines would be built, and how much the fares
would be. For the proponents of immediate municipal ownership, there was no such thing as just compensation for fran-

chises because no amount of money to the municipal government could assure a good transit system. As one of the mayor's backers put it, "If the voter is for private corporate control of the streets and street railways . . . he should vote for the election of Mr. Busse for mayor."[6]

A fair number of Chicagoans were sympathetic to this argument and fearful that the Republicans were in league with the companies currently holding traction franchises to get the best deal for the businessmen involved rather than for the people of the city. These fears had been apparent during past mayoral elections and at the charter convention, and the CFL had kept this issue on the agenda of its monthly meetings.[7] These suspicions about the motives of businessmen were furthered during the 1907 mayoral campaign when, a few days before the election, one of the franchise holders, the City Railway Company, announced pay raises for its employees if the traction agreements were ratified. The *Tribune* proclaimed that the way to this agreement "was paved by James Pease of the Republican county central committee and other friends of Mr. Busse."[8] Many Chicagoans would easily have believed this both of the Republican party and of Fred Busse. During his first term in the legislature, the mayoral candidate had voted to extend to ninety-nine years the traction franchises of Charles Yerkes.[9] Although Busse had reversed his position two years later, following public outrage over this deal, the image of him being sympathetic to franchise holders lingered in the minds of many Chicago voters.

Because the traction issue itself was inextricably involved in clashing visions about good municipal government as a whole, the arguments made by both sides during the mayoral campaign were not solely about municipal ownership, but rather about the future of the city itself. The newspaper coverage and speeches made during the campaign provide evidence for this. From the pages of the *Tribune*, the strongest supporter of the Republican cause among the city's dailies, emerged a tone of political hysteria conveying the sense that at least some Republicans believed Busse's election absolutely essential to reverse a trend in Chicago toward radical municipal government. Day after day during the campaign, the newspaper and its columnists and cartoonists vilified Dunne and anyone supporting him.[10] They linked Dunne to the political crusades of the "notorious" radical William Randolph Hearst, who, the paper warned, would come from New York to take control of Chicago if Dunne were reelected. State Lieutenant Governor Sherman gave a speech in Chicago denouncing Hearst and, by implication, Dunne and all his supporters as part of the lawless descendents of the worst elements of Haymarket.[11] In a poll the *Tribune* conducted among real-estate men, one respondent urged Busse's election because it would "settle for many years the question as to whether the long haired men and short haired women are going to rule and ruin this town." Thomas D. Knight repeated this theme when, presiding over a meeting of the Republican businessmen's Hamilton Club, he declared the club to be against the "long haired management of city affairs."

The newspaper mercilessly ridiculed Dunne and his campaign while extolling Busse's virtues. Headlines such as "Hysteria Rules Demo.-M. O. Camp" and "Dunne 'Loses' Use of Voice, Yet Abuses His Opponents" contrasted sharply with one proclaiming "Busse A Fighter: Credit to City."[12] The paper's cartoons depicted Dunne and his "cronies" hanging out the City Hall windows, all wild-eyed and long-haired. The convalescent Busse was shown reading in bed while "Democratic mudslingers" crept furtively beneath his window.[13]

The battle raging over reform of the public school system in early 1907 was set in this same context during the mayoral campaign. How to undertake this reform had been one of the most contentious questions considered by the charter convention. Now, the profound disagreements surrounding this issue—especially Mayor Dunne's appointments to the school board and the growing influence of the Chicago Federation of Teachers—flared anew and pitted businessmen against much of the rest of the city. On the one side stood those Chicagoans advocating a school system run by an all-powerful superintendent, preferably a businessman who would order the system around sound business principles with finances as the highest priority. Ranged against them were those people who believed that the teachers and the community as a whole should be given a greater measure of control by replacing the currently appointive board with an elective one and by according the teachers' union more say in the overall educational policy of the school system. Dunne's school board pointed decisively in the latter direction.

This unyielding conflict of ideas, the results of a nonbinding public-policy referendum in which the voters had registered their overwhelming favor of an elective board, and the vociferous rhetoric and determined actions of several convention delegates to implement an elective school board in the new charter, had intensified the alarm of the Chicago business community. The *Tribune* accused Dunne of having named a board of education composed "chiefly of avowed single taxers and socialists" and deplored the board's "plan to 'democratize' the school government" and "submit all questions of educational policy to the teachers."[14] Republicans accused the board of undertaking "one constant case of wild experiments and crank ideas" and of being run by "a preponderance of people with excessively progressive notions." What was needed instead, they declared, was "a good, straight, hard headed businessman like Mr. Busse to straighten out the muddle."[15]

The hysteria of this mayoral campaign was in large measure a legacy from Haymarket and the confrontations between business and the radical labor movement that had rocked the city during the last three decades of the nineteenth century. The distrust and hatred with which the two sides viewed each other were deeply ingrained in the political consciousness of the city. The hysteria also reflected the fears of more conservative Republicans that Dunne's reelection might guarantee municipal ownership and other municipal reforms that would reshape the city in ways to which they were unalterably opposed. The new charter and Busse in the mayor's office, these men hoped, would prevent this cataclysm. In a move that would only rebound against them in the future, they sought help for their cause from outside the city. Edward Shurtleff, the Republican Speaker of the House of Representatives from Marengo, Illinois, appeared as a featured speaker at several Busse rallies. Shurtleff called for Busse's election because he was the man to trust with the extended powers that the city would be granted by the new charter.[16] Having deferred to the state legislature repeatedly during the charter convention, the Republicans, with this additional alliance, were playing with fire. So many Chicagoans were already highly suspicious of the legislature's role in the new charter, and their hostility toward the legislature would only be inflamed by such overt links displayed during the mayoral campaign.

In the short term, the Republicans' gamble with Fred Busse paid off. On election day, they were victorious over Dunne and the Democrats by a margin of thirteen thousand votes. Their cause had undoubtedly been helped by Busse's German origin and his promise to the United Societies that, if elected, he would go to Springfield and fight for the separate bills drafted by the charter convention to give Chicago home rule on liquor regulation.[17] In the long run, their political cause would not be furthered. The positions they had staked out in the campaign against municipal ownership, against an elected school board and community participation in school decisions, and in favor of the charter, and the alliances they had made with the state legislators would come back to haunt them almost immediately after the election as the campaign to ratify the charter got underway. Nor did the malicious glee with which the *Tribune* crowed over Busse's victory go unnoticed or unanswered during the upcoming charter campaign. "Chicago," declared the newspaper, "has repudiated carpetbag government, puppet government, petticoat government, and pipe dream government. . . . The business and intelligent people have come into their own."[18]

The Charter Goes before the State Legislature

Following his election, Busse left for Springfield to fulfill his campaign pledge to lobby for passage of the charter and the liquor bills by the Illinois General Assembly. A delegation from the charter convention, others from Chicago civic and business groups, as well as representatives from the United Societies also descended upon Springfield. It quickly became clear to all these Chicagoans that the state legislature had its own ideas about acceptable charter legislation for Chicago and that this charter as written did not fit their bill. Before they even considered the charter itself, however, the legislators rejected the liquor bills. The House Charter Committee recommended against their passage and tabled the bills without discussion and without sending them to the full House. Representative McGoorty from Chicago, who had been a charter convention delegate, moved that the bills be reconsidered, but his motion was rejected and the United Societies returned to Chicago empty-handed.[19]

The charter's safe passage through the assembly was not assured either. When the charter was moved out of committee and placed before the assembly, downstate legislators demanded concessions from Chicago in return for its passage. These men were looking, as one student of Chicago-downstate relations put it, "upon the Chicago charter as a form of gift which should be traded for some other measure more desired by the country people."[20] The legislators were also thinking ahead to the 1910 census. Since this census would surely register still more population growth in Chicago, these men tried again to minimize the political damage to themselves by offering to trade the charter for permanent restriction on the number of representatives from Cook County. They hoped to limit Cook County to the nineteen senators and fifty-seven representatives accorded it by the 1901 reapportionment. But as had been the case often before, they could not muster the requisite two-thirds margin. The measure failed by a vote of twenty-seven to eighteen with the votes cast along regional lines: of the eighteen negative votes, fourteen came from Chicago and one from Cook County.[21] After failing in this tactic, the downstate legislators demanded that Chicago representatives support a new state-wide local option bill in return for the charter. This measure was the special project of Senator Orville Berry, a Republican from Carthage, Illinois, and chair of the Senate charter committee, and of the Anti-Saloon League, which had declared war against liquor in Chicago. This local option bill was intended to make it easier to accomplish total prohibition.[22] Believing they had little choice in the matter if they wished to see the charter pass, Chicago representatives either abstained or voted for the measure.

Passage of the local option bill, however, did not guarantee unimpeded passage of the charter through the legislature. Indeed, this body introduced several changes into the charter that would only serve to fuel the existing opposition in Chicago and clarify just exactly what various people in the city wanted from this charter.[23] Claiming the primacy of the state to decide election matters, the legislature eliminated the provision instituting the direct primary method for nominating candidates for municipal office and restored the old system of nomination by ward convention. The direct primary provision had been, for a variety of reasons, one of the most widely supported reform provisions of the charter: the Civic Federation reformers, for example, had seen it as a way to purge political corruption; the CFL had urged its inclusion in the charter to curb the power of the political bosses of both parties and thereby increase popular control of the political selection process and make political parties more responsible to the wishes of the people.[24] Now the state legislature put back into place the old system that most people, with the possible exception of some politicians, believed was corrupt.

In addition, the legislature rearranged the city's ward system, destroying the careful compromise the convention had reached over the number of wards and aldermen. Rather than ratifying the system of seventy wards with one alderman each drawn up by the convention, the new charter as amended gave the city fifty wards and fifty aldermen. This exact ward configuration had been specifically rejected by the convention delegates. As if this change was not outrageous enough, in the process of redrawing ward boundaries the legislature flagrantly gerrymandered the wards to create working-class Democratic wards with two and three times the population of obviously middle- and upper-class wards.

The amended version of the charter passed the Illinois House on May 7. After further tinkering by the Senate, the final version was ratified on May 12 and sent back to Chicago, where a referendum was scheduled for September 17.

The Purge of the Board of Education

In the meantime, Mayor Busse had returned to Chicago from Springfield and had taken up some unfinished business. He set about ousting ex-Mayor Dunne's appointees to the board of education. First, the mayor requested the resignations of twelve board members (at the time there were twenty-one members on the board), threatening to remove them if they failed to meet his demand. The immediate provocation for most of the dismissals was that these were board members unsympathetic to the current superintendent, and it was widely believed that they were planning to vote him out of the job the following month.[25] Raymond Robins and Louis Post were among the dismissed, as were two members of the Chicago Federation of Labor, John Sonsteby and John Harding. The latter was not among the original twelve, but as a board member described as voting "repeatedly for [Chicago] federation [of Teachers] measures," he soon followed.[26]

The *Tribune* was, of course, ecstatic with Busse's removals. Following the line it had pursued during the election campaign, the paper hailed the dismissals as a move that would "give the control of the city school system into the hands of a board dominated by a practical and capable business element."[27] Several of the dismissed board members refused to resign quietly, threatening to bring legal action against the mayor. But by the end of May, Busse had prevailed. His new appointees were exactly what his opponents had expected and feared: all were business and professional men. Two of these new appointees had also played important roles in developing the new charter's provisions on the school system. John R. Morrow was vice-president of the Merchants' Club and chair of its school committee; Theodore W. Robinson was vice-president of Illinois Steel and chair of the Chicago Commercial Association's educational committee. Another of the new board members, Chester M. Dawes, was a former member of the board who, during his previous tenure, had sponsored the prevailing requirement that the adoption of all textbooks and appointment of all teachers be approved by the superintendent. Upon receiving the news of his reappointment, he was quoted as saying, "I don't think the school teachers' union will last long under a new school board."[28]

Given the tension in the city regarding this issue, there was no way that Mayor Busse's actions on the school board could avoid becoming tied to the charter ratification process. The mayor violated everything that the CFL and other people in the city stood for by removing all the old board members who had supported the teachers' union and a more democratic school system and replacing them with antiunion businessmen who had already proclaimed fiscal efficiency as their primary objective. He also reinforced suspicions that the charter was a document designed to restructure the municipal government for the benefit of Republican politicians and businessmen. Even as he was being ousted from his seat on the school board, Louis Post was denouncing the charter as "a charter by politicians and corporations for politicians and corporations".[29]

FIVE

THE CAMPAIGN TO RATIFY THE CHARTER

In the wake of the shakeup of the board of education, and with the charter referendum scheduled for September 17, 1907, Chicagoans turned their attention to the charter. For the whole of the summer of 1907, Chicagoans listened to or read about debates on the charter and attended the numerous public and private meetings that were called to discuss the document. The CFL leadership authorized the appointment of special committees to begin studying all the provisions of the proposed charter so that the organization could make a recommendation to its membership. The Civic Federation began preparing a pamphlet explaining why the charter should be adopted and the City Club scheduled a series of discussions on various charter provisions. The Chicago Federation of Teachers, which was affiliated with, but not an official member of the CFL, declared against the charter and asked the CFL to support the teachers in this cause. The teachers also formed a committee of 250 that it authorized to work with women's suffrage organizations to defeat the charter. The Independence League and Louis Post began a series of articles and editorials in the *American* and in *The Public* denouncing the charter. Charles Merriam countered with articles in other papers, and Walter Fisher and Milton Foreman conducted their own campaigns for the charter. The United Societies scheduled its second annual convention for the last week of May and made the charter its main topic of discussion.[1] Thus, the arguments and interactions on the charter can be easily investigated because by the end of the summer Chicagoans had produced an amazing quantity of written material either denouncing or supporting the charter.

This chapter explores the ongoing disputes over several of the reform issues most in dispute at the convention—home rule, municipal revenues and taxation, the school system, the liquor question—in order to discover three things: first, to examine the continuity of the positions various Chicagoans had adopted toward the charter and its specific provisions; second, to look further at the ideas about municipal reform that had been developed by people throughout the city by late summer, and to show how these were cohesive ideas emanating from profoundly different views of good municipal government and of the city as a whole; and finally, to show to what extent the failure of Chicago's reform charter lay in the conflict between what people thought would result from this particular charter, and what they wanted to result from charter reform. The starting point is the ongoing argument among Chicagoans over whether this charter was a home-rule charter. For not only did this continue to be a rancorous issue, the disagreements on this question are a microcosm of the fundamentally different ways in which people had come to think about an urban environment.

What Is a Home Rule Government?

On June 14, the City Club of Chicago sponsored the first of three luncheon meetings to acquaint its members with specific provisions of the charter. The issue chosen for discussion at this first meeting was home rule. In the points made at this meeting, it becomes obvious that there existed among Chicagoans a fundamental difference of opinion as to what a home-rule government was, a difference of opinion that the CFL, United Societies, and various individuals had tried to explain months earlier to the charter convention.

The first of the featured speakers was Alderman Milton Foreman, chair of the late charter convention and avid supporter of the proposed charter. As he had done at the convention, Foreman spoke in the most authoritative of tones, preemptively dismissing any opposition to the charter. "Every feature of the charter that Chicago really wants," he told the audience, "is in the charter just as it was on the day it left the Charter convention." The legislature had altered nothing essential, he went on to assert, leaving "the charter for Chicago with the things in that Chicago, from an administrative and executive point of view, really wanted."[2]

Charles Merriam followed Foreman to the podium. Merriam was candid about the legislative changes, admitting that he did not like them and deploring the fact that the legislature refused to allow Chicago to make its own decisions on wards and election procedures. But he did not see that the changes were sufficient reason to turn down the charter, because, as he had told the convention, the major problems of the municipal government up to then had stemmed from the limited power and responsibility to act dictated by the old Cities and Villages Act. If the city passed the new charter, its home-rule provisions would remedy the situation. "Neither the retention of the convention system, nor the loss of the corrupt practices act, nor the ward reapportionment, can offset the tremendous advantage gained under such a [new charter] system."[3]

Despite the difference of opinion about the legislative changes to the charter, both Merriam and Foreman agreed that the charter was a home-rule charter. They could do so because the charter satisfied their particular and narrowly defined concept of home rule: by consolidating several overlapping administrative and taxing authorities into the municipal government, the proposed charter gave the city more actual decision-making and taxing powers than it had had previously. As Merriam stressed in his series of newspaper articles written later that summer, consolidation would place the entire bond debt under control of the municipal government, and this revision of the municipal revenue system would bring home rule to the city.[4] The same basic idea of home rule was held by most charter supporters. The Civic Federation, for example, simultaneously made this identical equation of consolidation and home rule. In the pamphlet it issued during the summer, the organization declared itself puzzled that some people could say they opposed the charter because it consolidated the parks into the municipal government and then proclaim that they wanted a real home-rule charter. How, the federation wondered, could this be?[5] The answer lies in the fact that there were different definitions of home rule. Home rule, to Merriam, Foreman, and the Civic Federation, meant consolidation because consolidation would have delineated clearer lines of municipal power and responsibility and would have provided for a more centralized and efficient government by the few at the top.[6] This type of home-rule structure was a fundamental part of their vision of good municipal government.

It was not, however, the only conceivable definition of home rule or of good municipal government, and other people in Chicago held a very different opinion. The final speaker at the City Club meeting, Edward Noonan, offered an opposing definition of home rule. Noonan was chief counsel of the United Societies and he disagreed totally with Foreman and Merriam about the home-rule aspects of the proposed charter. He now presented, for the first time to an audience outside of the United Societies, the reasons why the United Societies would oppose the charter. Noonan first took issue with the charges made by his fellow speakers and the daily newspapers that the United Societies had decided at its convention the month previous to fight the charter solely because it did not provide home rule on liquor. "That was not the case and it is not the fact. . . . nearly every speaker who addressed the convention stated other reasons . . . for opposing the charter. . . . The charter contains other provisions that are contrary to the wishes and the constitution of the United Societies."[7] Noonan explained to his audience that the United Societies had voted to oppose the charter because it created an entire scheme of government that the United Societies' membership and many other people in the city did not want. Part of that scheme was the limited home rule that the charter would confer. Home rule for the United Societies did not mean solely consolidated powers. The organization maintained that to introduce such a change without other signficant home-rule powers for the city would only produce a municipal government for the benefit of the corporations and the wealthy. Rather, a true home-rule government, as the United Societies had told the charter convention six months earlier, was a municipal government free from all the dictates of the rurally oriented, anti-Chicago state legislature, in which the people of the city held the power to determine their own laws.[8] Noonan reminded his listeners that this desire was definitely not limited to the United Societies. The people of Chicago had already expressed their wishes for such extensive home rule when they voted overwhelming in favor of propositions to institute the direct primary, elect the board of education, and adopt their own system of assessing and levying taxes.[9]

The United Societies therefore could not compromise with the charter as written; it could not, for instance, be satisfied that some home rule was better than none, because it rejected the very kind of home rule power this charter would confer upon the city. It feared the consolidation scheme not because it opposed centralized government, but because the type of centralized government contained in the charter was intended to deliver the city into the hands of only certain people.

In fact, if the men of the Civic Federation had understood the argument that the United Societies was making, they could have answered their own question about why the United Societies was not supporting this "home-rule" charter. However, a comparison between the Civic Federation's pamphlet on why the charter should be ratified and a pamphlet issued during the summer by the United Societies on why the charter should be rejected illustrates this absence of understanding. The Civic Federation pamphlet described the charter as a home-rule document because it "provides that the council may adopt an ordinance regulating . . . indeed any matter concerning which the charter makes provisions and regulations (*except* [italics mine] the provisions as to taxation, public utilities, school system, and any provisions expressly prohibiting the exercise of certain powers by the city)." [10] These elements that Foreman conceded were excluded from the city's home-rule powers, however, were precisely those home-rule powers that many Chicagoans wanted to secure for the municipal government. The United Societies pointed out in its pamphlet that the charter was not a home-rule document because home rule was not extended "to taxation, public utilities, the education system and all concerns which immediately touch the welfare of our Societies and the personal rights and freedoms of the people of Chicago." [11] In the context of the ongoing political conflicts within the city, and between city and state, the United Societies had come to believe that they as citizens had a right to determine how life in the city was to be lived. From this belief, the members of the United Societies had fashioned a view of home rule that demanded for the municipal government and for the voters the powers to decide on all purely municipal affairs. One of these municipal affairs, of course, was liquor regulation. And the United Societies could see no reason to support a charter that denied Chicagoans the type of government that they wanted and would "deny them the enjoyment of habits, manners and customs they have acquired for generations." [12] The state legislature's revision of the municipal ward system had given the United Societies further proof that this body could never be trusted to keep from interfering in municipal affairs. And any charter legislation that recognized the legal superiority of the state as clearly as this charter did risked forfeiting the prospect of self-government for the people of the city that the United Societies wanted them to have.

Viewed from the present, it may be hard to credit these people with having a different point of view that encompassed the whole city. But they were attempting to redefine urban government on the basis of what had come before them in the nineteenth century. From their perspective, a new-style, completely home-rule government was every bit as valid as the limited, consolidation-oriented home-rule reform advocated by the supporters of the charter. Moreover, the latter type of reforms, where they were implemented, did necessarily distinguish themselves as providing good government. [13] What is relevant is that many of the opponents of the charter had conceptualized municipal government and the city as a whole in a way that conflicted with the views of those backing the charter.

Is the City Simply a Business Arena?

The discussions surrounding the issues of municipal revenue and taxation highlight these differing conceptions. The second charter discussion hosted by the City Club in late June of 1907 specifically addressed these matters. Conspicuously absent from this gathering were any speakers opposing the charter on this question. Two of the three speakers were former charter convention members who wholeheartedly supported the charter and its revenue provisions. Frank I. Bennett, who also chaired the City Council Finance Committee, lauded the charter because consolidation would provide Chicago with more revenue, and "in order to have a better and greater Chicago there must needs be more money." But although everyone might agree that more municipal revenue was desirable, the crucial question was where the money would come from. Bennett and cospeaker Frank L. Shepard particularly stressed how the new charter would set specific tax limits that could not be raised by state laws. They also claimed that it would increase the level of bond indebtedness and thereby provide a means to avoid raising property taxes. The charter, according to Shepard, would mean "a definite, precise and permanent, and at the same time conservative tax limitation for the taxpayer, a limitation calculated to encourage prospective investors in homes and property in this community." The third speaker, Nathan MacChesney (attorney for the real estate board), reiterated this theme, linking the interests of the City of Chicago with "a reasonable tax limitation, and that limitation is necessary because no man will invest in Chicago, and no man will feel safe in owning in Chicago, unless he can be sure that the tax will not be so high as to practically amount to confiscation." [14]

These men were property owners and property-tax payers; as Clifton Yearley pointed out several years ago, for men such as these, protecting themselves against paying excessive taxes was a vital component of their reform ideal. [15] Thus, the proposed charter was the perfect vehicle for these men. It would have limited the taxes they might themselves have to pay and would have provided an alternative means for raising the municipal revenues that they knew the city had to have, and simultaneously it would have placed control of the political machinery, especially the fiscal decision making, more tightly in their own hands to insure that the system ran smoothly.[16]

In their presentations to the City Club, Shepard, Bennett, and MacChesney were echoing the sentiments expressed by the Civic Federation when it proclaimed that the charter as written was a good piece of reform legislation precisely because of its revenue provisions. The charter, according to the Civic Federation, would set a ceiling on taxation, would judiciously extend the city's borrowing power which in turn would make the city a better and more desirable place to live and do business and consequently enhance property values, and would bring greater "efficiency and economy in administration" to the municipal government.[17]

Since the City Club did not invite representatives of opposing viewpoints, one must turn to different sources to find what these were. By late July, it had become obvious to the CFL, the United Societies, and the Independence League that the businessmen of the reform organizations wanted to use the charter both to control municipal taxation for the benefit of corporations and property investors and to prevent radical government from ever coming to Chicago. The Civic Federation certainly did nothing to dispel this perspective when it denounced all criticism of the charter as selfish, blatantly political, or "uttered by persons of unsafe theories and principles," criticisms "such as might be expected from socialist newspapers and socialist street corner harangues."[18]

The internal committee commissioned by the CFL leadership to study the charter provisions reported its conclusions in mid-July. Its final report scathingly denounced the charter supporters for attempting to control the municipal government for their own benefit. Charging that the document was supported by "all the predatory, tax-dodging, labor baiting interests . . . who fear the rule by the whole people [and] seek to curb the power of the electorate,"[19] the report painted a bleak picture of the kind of municipal government controlled by the few for the benefit of the few that would result if this charter were adopted. The report singled out the charter's revenue provisions as designed to place a disproportionate share of the tax burden on the renters and small property owners, while allowing the wealthy and the corporations to evade paying their fair share of taxes. The charter's provision allowing special assessments for property owners for street and sidewalk repairs was cited as an example of this imbalance. The charter specified that the city would pay for first-time improvements, after which property owners would be assessed 50 percent of the cost for subsequent repairs to streets and sidewalks. Louis Post had argued in vain at the convention that the municipal government should assume the burden of paying for these improvements because the city as a whole benefited from them, because wealthy property owners could afford the assessment more easily than small-property owners, and because renters, who had no property value to be increased by such improvements, always had the cost of special assessments passed on to them by their landlords. The convention had rejected these arguments, but now, during the campaign, they were resurrected by the CFL.[20]

The CFL report cited several other critically objectionable municipal features that would result from this charter. The school system, it warned, would become "a cog in the capitalistic machine so that the children may reach manhood's estate, content in a condition of abject servitude"; progressive reforms such as the initiative and direct primary were completely lacking; and there would be no implementation of municipal ownership. In short, the committee summarized, the charter contains "nothing that will give the people better control of their own affairs . . . nothing to preserve the liberties of the people against the encroachments of concentrated wealth and plutocratic greed."[21] After listening to the report, the CFL leadership accepted the committee's recommendation to reject the charter and vowed to conduct an all-out campaign of opposition. For the rest of the summer, the charter remained one of the CFL's chief topics of discussion and planning as the organization continued to investigate the charter's various provisions and hone its position. At its first meeting of August, the CFL leadership announced that it would furnish anticharter speakers to any local requesting them and added to the objections it had already raised against the charter the warning that several other provisions could be used directly by business to control laborers.[22]

Joining the CFL in developing a coherent stance against the charter was the Independence League, a reform group affiliated with William Randolph Hearst. The arguments about good urban reform that were proposed by the Independence League have generally been ignored by historians in recent years, but its ideas were at one time taken quite seriously. Indeed, they furnished the original historical interpretation of the Progressive Era, namely the analysis drawn from these ideas by the "Progressive" historians that the era was characterized by a struggle between the people and special interests.[23] However, subsequent historians rejected this analysis, replacing it first with a liberal consensus interpretation,[24] and then with reform theories based on categories and models of reformers. In the process, the ideas and arguments of groups such as the Independence League were consigned to irrelevancy. Yet, in Chicago, the Independence League held very definite opinions of what would make for a good overall municipal government.[25] When its ideas are placed into the city's political context, they fit logically and clearly into the fabric of the urban reform politics of the time.

The fiscal provisions of the proposed charter, in particular, incensed the Independence League. As an examination of their arguments will show, the men of the Independence League based their ideas on the concept that owners of private property had obligations to the city as a whole. But their understanding of this concept sprang not from a sense of a new wealthy, middle-class *noblesse oblige*, as one recent study concluded, but from the idea that the wealthy and powerful property owners were the obstacles to the development of a good urban community, and that a primary purpose of reform ought to be making them fulfill their obligations.[26]

In a series of articles in the Chicago *American*,[27] the Independence League outlined its ideas. It accused the charter conven-

tion of having conspired with big business to design a charter for
their own political and economic benefit—an argument not unlike that of the CFL—and denounced the charter for having as
one of its primary functions the aim of helping the wealthy
evade their responsibilities to society. According to the league,
one of the chief reasons why cities did not have enough capital
to function properly was that those with the most wealth contributed proportionately the least back to the community as a
whole. "Tax dodgers and privilege seekers have coiled their
leechlike tentacles around Chicago's vitals these many years.
There is not a scintilla of relief from these parasites in the new
charter"; [28] "the kings of Packingtown, convicted of a thousand
offenses against the public from whom they derive their revenue, are near the head of the list of tax-dodgers, of course," and
"the corporate gang of freebooters demand the new charter
which would increase taxation to the poor." [29] Such declarations
abound in the articles in the *American*. The paper particularly
accused International Harvester (the former McCormick Reaper
Works of Haymarket infamy) of dodging $2.1 million in taxes,
money that "could educate 75,000 children or raise firemen's
pay, clean streets, open parks, build more public baths, pay
policemen more." [30]

Perhaps it was this stridency and overblown hyperbole that
contributed to the rejection of the league's ideas by later historians. But, the rhetoric of the Independence League reveals a
core of ideas about the problems facing early-twentieth-century
cities. It is obvious in the specifics they named that they believed
in the responsibility of municipal governments to provide and
finance essential public services—schools, police and fire protection, transit—and that the question they asked in this regard
was the same as that asked by businessmen reformers: from
where was the money to come? Their answer of course was different. The Independence League believed that the wealthy, especially the wealthy corporations, were failing to meet their social obligation to the community as a whole, leaving the city
woefully short of revenue. "On one hand," the *American* edi-
torialized, "there are closed vacation schools, abominably filthy
streets, underpaid police and firemen and countless public defi-

ciencies because of lack of revenue. On the other hand . . . there are hundreds of millions of dollars worth of property on which no assessment has been levied and on which no tax has been collected."[31] Without a dramatic change in this situation, there could be no adequate municipal reform, no possibility of creating a decent urban environment for the majority of people.

Considering the fact that this same argument is made today by people incensed at the tax write-offs and loopholes that enable the major corporations of the country to pay little or no taxes, the ideas of the Independence League eighty years ago ought to be accorded more credence. Today these are not merely complaints about big guys versus little guys, and they were not that simplistic in the Progressive Era either. The theme is a recurrent one in American history: it is a denunciation of the ethos of the American capitalist system. But recognition of the theme without an investigation of what people do with the theme tells us really very little of importance. For the members of the Independence League, what is crucial is that this particular view of society shaped their ideas about good urban government and determined what remedies they offered for reform. Using the analysis of urban reform that has often been proposed, that of dividing businessmen into two categories, the old businessmen, who opposed reform, and the new-style middle-class businessmen, who led the progressive reform movements, also obscures the ideas of the Independence League.[32] The perspective of the Independence League was that they were all businessmen engaged in reshaping the city for their own benefit.

The urban reform ideas that the Independence League developed thus emanated from a sense that the current municipal system did not work primarily because the people who could most afford to help make it work were refusing to pay. When it came to charter reform, therefore, they conceived of a much different solution for the city's problems than the charter proposed to bring. Not only were many of the people most involved in writing the charter those who, according to the Independence League, had heretofore refused to pay their share; the new Chicago charter, the league charged, was the calculated attempt of corporations and businessmen to restructure a municipal government that would firmly place the financial burden of running the city somewhere else, and, even worse, would allow them to make money off of it. In allowing the city to issue more municipal bonds, the new charter would increase the potential of one segment of the urban community for investing in and deriving income from municipal improvements.[33] The Independence League did not stand alone in this perspective. The CFL was making a similar argument, and so was the United Societies. Among the reasons that the United Societies gave for rejecting the charter was that it would allow the "rich [to] conceal their money in hand and bonds and securities, and the powerful corporations [to], as usual, avoid the taxation."[34]

Similar to the arguments made by the advocates of municipal ownership that good public utilities could never be assured as long as they were seen primarily as money-making ventures rather than as absolutely necessary public services, the Independence League, the CFL, and the United Societies rejected the idea that a major city could or should rely so heavily on voluntary investment of businessmen in that city's upkeep. As proof of its allegations that this was a charter designed specifically to benefit the business community, the Independence League charged Milton Foreman, who had assumed the leading role in the procharter campaign, with calling for business to contribute at least $100,000 to the cause for fear that, if the charter lost, a constitutional convention would result which would cause a drastic change in the tax laws. Foreman was quoted as saying that "it would be cheaper for the corporations to put up $50,000,000 than to suffer a constitutional convention."[35]

That the "radical" ideas of the Independence League and of its patron William Randolph Hearst terrified a considerable number of Chicago businessmen had been apparent during the recent mayoral campaign. The *Tribune* had warned its readers that Edward Dunne was a stooge of Hearst, and that a vote for Dunne was a vote for Hearst and anarchy.[36] One speaker at a campaign rally for Busse had called the race a contest between the forces of good and evil. Busse, he said, belonged to the camp of Theodore Roosevelt, around whom "gather the strong, the virtuous, and the brave of the nation, while beneath the crossbones and skull of the Mephistopheles of yellow journalism [that is, Hearst] is massed an amalgamated, hybernated, conglomerate constituency, typical of envy, passion, hatred, and the spirit of socialistic agitation, and revolution."[37] Strong words and strong passions for a mayoral campaign, they indicated the deep fear and hatred with which city residents could view each other at this time. The Dunne supporters could not be comforted either by the veiled threats issued by State Lieutenant Governor Sherman, who, when speaking at another Busse rally, equated a vote for Dunne with a vote to return to the lawless era of Haymarket and promised that if that came about, the forces of the law would react as they did before. "It will not be the first time that a Chicago jury has passed on . . . the disease of lawlessness," remarked Sherman, "the disease that in an aggravated form produced the Haymarket riots. And those paid the penalty and were cured of their disease on the gallows."[38]

However, the men who belonged to the Independence League were neither crackpots nor the lawless anarchists that the *Tribune* would have had the city believe. Most of them were solid professionals, many of them lawyers. But in the context of Chicago's political culture they had developed ideas about municipal government different from those of the businessmen in the civic organizations. They feared and hated each other's motives: just as the CFL and the business community could find no common ground on which to compromise over municipal affairs or just as United Societies distrusted the motives of men whom they believed in league with state politicians.

Opposition to the Charter from Other Quarters

By the middle of the summer, the prospects for the charter had turned decisively dimmer as opposition to it spread among Chicago residents. Sometimes working through organizations, sometimes speaking as individuals, more and more Chicagoans joined the anticharter crusade as the campaign progressed. Their opposition hinged on a variety of reasons, but sprang generally from the same source: the belief that the restructured municipal government provided by the charter was not the one they wanted. Many women in Chicago, for instance, were sorely disappointed that the charter convention had refused to grant municipal suffrage in the proposed charter. Without this right, women believed they lacked the means for reshaping the city and for controlling their own affairs. Now many of them decided to work against the charter.

As was often the case with anything involving women, the newspapers neglected to pay much attention to women's opinions about the charter. The *American* probably gave the best coverage to their involvement in the charter campaign, proclaiming that "Chicago's best women have enlisted in the wide-sweeping anti-charter campaign." The paper quoted one member of the women's anticharter campaign as explaining "the women of Chicago are not indifferent to Chicago's welfare. By painful roundabout efforts they have initiated much public improvement. . . . We have patiently used our antiquated, clumsy, labor-wasting methods of meeting our needs. We now demand a modern implement—the ballot."[39] The vote would cut out the political and sometimes marital gameplaying and pleading for favors that they were currently forced to undertake in order to implement the changes they desired in the city. The way this game had to be played was portrayed by Louise DeKoven Bowen, a prominent Chicago woman much involved in various reform projects in the city. In her autobiography, *Growing Up with a City*, she told the story of how the law to add probation officers to the Juvenile Court was finally passed in Illinois because she had made a personal appeal to a "noted Illinois politician." Her friend, she related, "called up one of the bosses of the Senate and one in the House," and told each of them to see that the law was passed. When these two men asked what was in the bill, Bowen's friend replied "there is nothing in it, but a woman I know wants it passed." Having the law enacted in this fashion gave Bowen "a feeling of great uneasiness."[40]

The same irritation was felt increasingly by women throughout the city who were finding the distance between themselves and the political arena more and more intolerable. Women workers, for instance, were tired of having to plead with male unions to stand up for them in both union and municipal affairs. Union member Elizabeth Maloney told a meeting of the Women's Trade

Union League at Hull-House that working women could not afford to have the charter pass because they "will lose the opportunity of securing suffrage for twenty years."[41] Jane Addams summed up the feeling of many women. Recalling the variety and number of women who had petitioned for the charter to grant them municipal suffrage, and the reasons they gave for wanting this political power, Addams observed that it "seemed as if the time must be ripe for political expression of that public concern on the part of women which had so long been forced to seek indirection. . . . [to] seek an opportunity to cooperate directly in civic life through the use of the ballot in regard to their own civic affairs."[42] The charter without the municipal vote violated women's broader vision of their place, function, and rights in urban society. Without the vote, they knew that they stood little chance of implementing their visions of good municipal government or of stopping the visions of people to whom they were opposed.[43]

One Chicagoan who carried on a citizen's crusade against the charter was Raymond Robins, a social worker and a respected figure in Chicago. He belonged to several municipal clubs and organizations, he had been a delegate to the charter convention, and he had served on the board of education. Robins is a Progressive Era figure labeled too easily with the tag of "social reformer" by those who have interpreted urban reform movements as possessing a dichotomy between social and structural reformers.[44] But, while Robins did indeed have a vision of social reform for Chicago, it is doubtful that he himself would have separated social and structural reform from one another. They were two sides of the same coin: structural reform of the municipal government that placed responsibility for municipal affairs squarely in the city council with strong provisions for popular referendum would make social reform possible. Thus, he had willingly participated in the charter convention, advocating a strong home-rule government, municipal ownership, the initiative and referendum, among other reforms.[45] Although Robins was sorely disappointed with much of the charter as written, he did not adopt his firm anticharter stance until the state legislature made its changes to the charter. These changes, combined

with the defects that he believed already existed, served to turn
him decisively against the charter, for his vision of the proper
ends of structural reform differed from that of most charter
supporters.

Throughout the summer of 1907, Robins campaigned inde-
fatigably across the city against the charter, never as the spokesperson for any particular group, but always because he objected
strenuously to the municipal government as it would be restructured under the proposed charter. He defined the disagreements
over the charter as a struggle between two principles: that of
widening popular control over municipal government to achieve
equal rights among the citizenry versus a narrowing of municipal powers to gain class control through special privileges.[46]
Robins definitely believed that the charter embodied the latter
principle, and, in a speech given to the Public Policy League in
late July, he attacked the charter for extending to a restructured
government the wrong powers designed for the benefit of the
wrong people. The legislators, he told his audience, had destroyed any chance of effective housing reform in the city by removing the provision giving the city council power to enforce the
tenement ordinances; the limited home-rule provisions gave the
people little or no voice in the government; the school system
would be guided by people interested only in fiscal rather than
educational matters; and the revenue provisions were designed
to ensure "that millions of dollars of income-paying property es-
capes taxation, that small property owners pay more taxes in
proportion than larger property owners, and that much of the
city's present income is squandered by venal and incompetent
officials."[47] The charter, he told another anticharter gathering
that month, had become the "deformed product of political and
business thieves."[48]

The Charter and Politics

As the charter drew more opposition and more stinging accusations that the proposed scheme of municipal government
promoted political and economic favoritism, its supporters responded in increasingly strident manner. They warned voters
that to reject the charter would bring more woes down upon

their heads than they had now. Many of these warnings were actually threats, often made by state legislators, that the city would suffer retaliation from the state if it failed to pass this charter. In mid-July, at the third City Club meeting that had as its topic the political features of the charter, two of the three speakers were state legislators: James Kittleman (Republican representative from the Chicago suburb of Berwyn) and Morton D. Hull (Republican of Chicago). Their comments and those of the third speaker, Harold Ickes, provide the context for examining the kinds of threats made against Chicago voters.

Turning to the speeches of Kittleman and Hull at the City Club, one sees first the kind of threats they were making. Kittleman predicted that if the charter failed now, the city would have to reconcile itself never to have any home-rule powers because it would probably never again receive so generous a grant of municipal powers from the legislature as that contained in this charter. Hull reinforced his fellow legislator's warnings, saying that the only reason Chicago had obtained this charter in the first place was that the legislators traded it for the local option bill. "If they reject this charter," he told the audience, "and go back again for another charter . . . they will probably have to pay a price for it, and that price will be a permanent restriction of the representation of Cook County in the General Assembly."[49]

Kittleman then dismissed the idea that the city might have any legitimate grievance against the changes made in Springfield on any of the charter's provisions. Neither the ward restructuring nor the removal of the direct primary, Kittleman admonished the audience, had any bearing on the charter's worthiness.[50] In addition, he attacked all suggestions that partisan politics had played any role in the charter movement. He praised the state legislature for not letting partisan politics interfere in their decisions over the charter, saying that both Democrats and Republicans had concurred over removal of the direct primary provision and redistricting the wards.[51]

However, for Chicago's residents, the role of political parties and political bosses in the charter campaign was an important issue. One of the central themes of Progressive Era history has been the desire of urban reform movements to eradicate political corruption and political party bosses. But, because the focus of study has been on a particular group of city residents, the extent to which this distrust of politics and political bosses touched all groups and classes of urban society has been undervalued. Although some historians using the ethnocultural approach have recognized this distrust of politicians, at least as a motivating factor behind the desire for the reforms of initiative, referendum, and recall, they have tended to assume that the people they study were unquestioning supporters of the bosses of political parties. Ethnic voters, historians have perceived, stuck with politicians whom they perceived as willing to give them "material goods, recognition, and defense of their cultural heritage" in return for votes.[52]

But the arguments made by many Chicagoans against the political ramifications of the charter do not support this conclusion. Chicagoans, in fact, attacked the charter's political features because they saw the charter as too much the product of all politicians, state and city, Democratic and Republican, getting together and carving up Chicago for their own purposes. The legislature's redistricting of the wards and the apparent equanimity with which most politicians accepted this furnished proof to them that the charter contained too many concessions to political bossism. Many people in Chicago genuinely believed that the new four-year term for aldermen, the way the wards were gerrymandered, and the fifty smaller wards with only one alderman apiece would make it easier for political parties and business to control elections and the City Council. Harold Ickes stressed these fears in his response to Kittleman at the City Club. "Small wards," he warned, "will result in making it easier for the machine politician to control." There was also more safety, he thought, in two aldermen per ward with shorter terms. "It would be more difficult for the ward boss to nominate, elect and control two aldermen than one alone . . . [and] the longer the term of a public official the less sense does he have of responsibility to the people."[53]

In his remarks, Ickes deviated from the position of Charles Merriam, with whom he agreed on many other reform issues. Other opponents of the charter agreed with Ickes. The CFL charged that the four-year term "removes the public servant further from the voter" and gives him "plenty of time for graft," while maintenance of the old primary system "leaves candidate selection to the bosses."[54] The United Societies protested the arrogance of the politicians in redistricting the wards, a move that would make it easier for corporations to corrupt the city council.[55] Raymond Robins objected to the reinstitution of the "old gang primary law," and Louis Post and the Independence League made similar protests.[56]

The arguments of the opponents of the charter also contradict the theories advanced in previous studies of Chicago politics that ethnic groups in the city feared civil service because it "would prevent them from getting city jobs" and that they opposed the direct primary because they agreed with Republican boss William Lorimer that "the direct primary would militate against 'representation of the different subdivisions, geographically, or by the different nationalities.'"[57] Far from opposing the direct primary, both the United Socities and CFL actively supported this reform. Before the charter convention had convened, the CFL had passed a resolution to this effect. "Whereas the popular control of the primaries and a secret ballot is essential to free government and the welfare of the people, [be it resolved that] plurality vote shall nominate and nominating conventions be abolished."[58] The CFL supported the direct primary because it believed that such a reform would help protect the people against corrupt politicians. Within Chicago's political context, the CFL's promotion of direct primary reform was an essential part of its entire vision of reforming the municipal government.

The same idea is true of the stand taken by various charter opponents toward the civil-service provisions of the charter. Rather than opposing civil-service reforms per se, the CFL, the United Societies, and former Mayor Dunne fought the partial civil-service reform embodied in the revised charter which specifically exempted the public school teachers, department heads, and the municipal court employees. They charged that the charter's civil-service provision would not eliminate political corruption and favoritism altogether, but would only shift it to benefit other groups in the city.[59] It is easier to credit these arguments as something other than rhetorical devices if they are not viewed backwards from the present where subsequent decades have shaped and hardened political attitudes, but rather as Chicagoans in 1907 saw the situation based on what had preceded them in the nineteenth century.

The Civic Federation doubted the sincerity of these claims. The organization accused those in the city who spoke against the charter over the issue of the direct primary as being from "quarters that have not heretofore shown enthusiasm in primary reform of any kind."[60] But the evidence proves the Civic Federation wrong. Some Democratic politicians did oppose the charter for personal reasons; for example, ward bosses Johnny Powers and Michael Kenna feared losing their wards to the redistricting. But not all Democratic bosses felt that way, for the Independence League accused some Democratic aldermen of disrupting anticharter meetings and party boss Roger Sullivan of giving only token opposition to the charter,[61] and in any case those Democrats who most vociferously opposed it were from the radical Dunne wing of the party. They did so because the restructured municipal government would promote political bossism, would put businessmen and their political henchmen in control of the schools, would not implement home rule or provide for municipal ownership, and would not give the people more control over the municipal government.[62] Dunne's opposition to the charter on these grounds was certainly genuine; he had always promoted this political platform.[63] And it was Dunne and his allies who kept the party on a vigorous anticharter course because, despite losing the mayor's office, they retained control of the Cook County Democratic Central Committee.[64]

To a great extent the question many Chicagoans were asking themselves as they studied the charter was the one put to the City Club by Harold Ickes. Should the voters of Chicago "accept this charter notwithstanding its defects and in spite of the fact that it appears to deliver us bound hand and foot into the power of the professional politician . . . which in its political aspects is a boss rule charter?"[65] In view of the city's past history of collusion between politicians and businessmen on labor issues and the franchise question, it is not surprising that the political features of the proposed charter should have been greeted so skeptically by the majority of the citizenry. And neither Dunne's views on the charter nor those of the CFL or the United Societies can be dismissed as mere political rhetoric. Previous evidence also exists to support the idea that the majority of Chicagoans opposed political bossism as it existed in Chicago at the turn of the century. The success of the MVL's political reform campaigns, in which their candidates failed only in the most egregiously boss-run wards, is one strong example of this.[66]

The question that remains to be asked is why the Civic Federation did not object to the political changes made in the charter by the legislature. The very fact that the Civic Federation did not care that the direct primary provision was removed from the charter strongly supports the idea that what they were most interested in was not nonpartisan politics but municipal politics controlled by Republicans. For Republican politicians, the ward redistricting and the removal of the direct primary, despite the protestations of Kittleman to the contrary, seemed to assure them control of the city.[67] Some of the nonpoliticians supporting the charter—men such as Walter Fisher and Charles Merriam, for example—were less cynical. Nevertheless, from everything that most charter supporters said and did it is evident that they claimed nonpartisanship because they did not think they were politically motivated. They were so certain that what they wanted was right that they could not see it as a political stance. The CFL, the United Societies, and other people in the city never forgot that they were dealing with a political situation and that every position adopted was a political one.

Blinded to opposing viewpoints by their belief that they were simply promoting the most righteous cause, the charter's supporters made another blunder when they brought state politicians into the city to speak for the charter. By reminding Chicago of the local option bill and its relationship to the charter and by resurrecting at the same time the issue of home-rule powers and state control of municipal affairs, state legislator Morton Hull had thrown more kindling into the anticharter fire. Charter supporters continued to show their insensitivity when, in August, they invited downstate legislators to address groups of charter supporters. Early that month, both Orville Berry, the sponsor of the local option bill, and Speaker of the House Edward Shurtleff, who had campaigned in Chicago for Mayor Busse's election the previous spring, spoke before the Hamilton Club. Berry threatened Chicagoans that if they did not pass the charter, they could expect no essential or desirable laws out of the state legislature in their lifetime.[68]

Shurtleff compounded Berry's offensiveness by assuring the Hamilton Club that if the city voted against the charter it would be conclusive proof that the city did not know how to govern itself. Not content with this insult, however, Shurtleff gave charter opponents even further ammunition when he told the club that this was a true home-rule charter because it provided municipal self-government for everything except the school system, taxation, and public utilities.[69] If the United Societies, the CFL, the Independence League, and other people in the city needed further evidence that the charter supporters and the state legislators thought alike about home rule, here it was. Shurtleff had used the very same examples as the Civic Federation in its pamphlet, and these, of course, were exactly the areas where the charter opponents wanted to gain strong home-rule powers in a new charter.

The United Societies had not forgotten the active part Shurtleff had taken in Mayor Busse's election campaign a few months earlier when he had called the Republican candidate the man to trust "with the extended power contained in that charter."[70] This past arrangement seemed all the more important now because the mayor firmly supported the charter and was threatening to exercise these new powers to regulate liquor. In early September, Busse accused the United Societies of being in league with the saloonkeepers and brewery interests of the city to oppose the charter because it did not grant home rule on liquor. The mayor threatened to implement state laws on Sunday closings immediately if the charter were defeated.[71] The German newspapers objected vehemently to his accusations of colluding with the brewers and of having a one-issue opposition to the charter. They advised their readers to ignore Busse's threats and to vote against the charter, based on the principles already defined by the United Societies.[72] Under these circumstances, it is easy to see why the Societies saw collusion between the Republican mayor, his party, Republican businessmen, and state politicians to control Chicago for their benefit while ignoring the wishes of the majority of the citizens.

The appearances of Berry and Shurtleff before the Hamilton Club, the mayor's statements, and several incidents as the campaign drew to a close helped complete for the anticharter forces the picture they had been drawing of a restructured municipal government under the new charter: a government dominated by the few in the city and under the thumb of the state government. Charter opponents accused the mayor of dispatching the police force to raid peaceful anticharter gatherings and the post office (until five months earlier, Busse had been postmaster of Chicago and had virtually designated his successor) with not delivering anticharter literature.[73] Then, almost as if it wished to justify the fears of charter opponents, in the final days before the referendum, the Republican-controlled board of elections reversed its earlier ruling on the type of election this was. Previously, the board had decided that the referendum was a general election, and under this ruling the city had been required to hold a special registration day. Now, just before the actual voting day, the board decided that this was a "special" election, even though it had already printed and distributed to polling places fliers proclaiming this a general election. The distinction was a crucial one. In a general election, employers were required to grant employees two hours off (without pay) in which to vote; for a special election, this privilege did not prevail. The United Societies quickly sent a letter of protest to the board, charging it with attempting to disfranchise the labor vote. But the board held firm in its decision.[74] The *American* declared the board's last minute reversal a blatant ploy to disfranchise workers and anticharter voters, conceived only after it finally realized the size of the anticharter forces.[75]

In the final weeks of the charter campaign, both sides stepped up their activities and speechmaking. For the anticharter forces, ex-mayor Edward Dunne, alderman William Dever, and Democratic party chairman William O'Connell spent the week before the referendum reiterating the party's official anticharter position.[76] The Independence League held a series of last minute rallies condemning the charter for selling "the future benefits of [the] children to a few men who will do nothing else but further their own selfish interests" and for leaving the "Springfield bosses" in control of the city.[77] The CFL was confident of the charter's defeat and was working on a strategy for calling a constitutional convention as the method for achieving charter reform.[78]

The United Societies held an anticharter rally and picnic at Riverview Amusement Park two Sundays before the referendum and sent speakers to the meetings of various ethnic societies in the closing weeks of the campaign.[79] But the climax of its anticharter campaign was an outdoor rally in Grant Park, just east of the city's downtown business district, on the Sunday preceding the referendum. The rally drew more than thirty thousand people. Half of them had assembled beforehand at various points near downtown and paraded through the streets with banners, flags, and marching bands. Speakers at the rally stressed once again the United Societies' main points of opposition: the taxation scheme "deprived the masses for the benefit of the few because what really was needed was a scheme to compel all to pay their fair share"; Sunday closings were sure to result from this charter; and the ward redistricting "deprived the working man of his vote."[80]

For the other side, the charter's supporters also worked up to the last minute to convince the voters to ratify the charter. But, as usual, the words they chose were hardly designed to appeal to the people most opposed to it. Mayor Busse urged ratification because "the best thought of the best citizenship in this community approves the Charter. It is demanded by the press, the pulpit, the commercial and industrial interests."[81] Except for the *American* and *Inter-Ocean*, the major newspapers supported the charter and used similar rhetoric. The *Tribune* urged acceptance of the charter because the "real estate owner will find in [it] his best guarantee against excessive taxation," and the day before the referendum, the paper printed a front-page cartoon with a hand labeled "Progressive Citizen" casting an affirmative vote and bearing the caption "Tonight the city will know whether it is under the control of progressives or reactionaries." The *Daily News* characterized charter opposition as "part of the world-wide opposition to progress, stirred up by interests which operate best under weak, disorderly, and confused government." The *Record-Herald* adopted a more conciliatory voice, admitting that the political changes were regrettable, but saying that all in all the good points of the charter clearly outweighed the bad and that it should therefore be ratified.[82]

On September 17, 1907, the Chicago voters went to the polls to register their opinions on the new proposed municipal charter. They rejected the charter by a vote of 121,935 to 59,786. Only four of the city's thirty-five wards ratified the charter, and two of those wards contained a high number of Republican middle- and upper-class voters. Mayor Busse's ward turned down the charter.[83]

SIX

FAILURE AND AFTERMATH

Chicagoans chose not to accept the reform charter in 1907. The reasons for their choice emanated directly from the city's political culture. The losers in this contest, however, did not understand this fact. In the days following the referendum, they responded to their defeat with a mixture of bitterness and resignation that displayed little understanding for the concerns and differing ideas that their opponents had expressed and the fact that these had led directly to the charter's defeat. A sorely disappointed Walter Fisher, who only days before had confidently expected the people to reject political bosses by ratifying the charter,[1] charged that the charter had been beaten by a "combination of selfishness and stupidity with which every constructive movement has to contend."[2] His assumption, of course, had been that his definition of political bosses and of the method to eliminate them was the only true one.

The assessments of the major newspapers were in line with their prereferendum opinions. The *Tribune* was vitriolic, declaring that, in turning down the charter, the city had proved that "it does not want home rule . . . that it does want a patchwork of taxing bodies . . . that it does not want uniformity, efficiency, and sanity in government."[3] As it had done during the campaign, the more moderate *Record-Herald* attempted to present a more even-handed account of the defeat. The paper attributed the loss to the citizens' fears of increased taxation and Sunday closings.[4]

Even with the passage of time, after the bitter taste of defeat had had time to dissipate, charter supporters remained unable to credit their opponents with having honest or worthy motives. One month after the vote, in a letter explaining the charter's failure, Charles Merriam credited its opponents with having seriously believed that increased taxation and Sunday closings would have resulted from the proposed charter. Yet he continued to think that these were unwarranted and irrational fears. As he termed it, "political juggling" had organized and played upon these fears and thus was responsible for the charter's demise. Moreover, he professed himself still unable to comprehend why men such as Louis Post and Raymond Robins had opposed the charter.[5] In his assessment of the movement some months later, the former charter convention chairman Milton Foreman displayed the same lack of understanding. According to Foreman, the charter failed because of the "intrusion of subsidiary issues and not by reason of any defect in it as a working organic law for the municipality."[6]

The charter's opponents were of course jubilant in their victory; and they took their opportunity in the spotlight to repeat that they had opposed this particular charter and not reform itself. Even as Walter Fisher and others were declaring the charter's defeat a result of selfish, partisan politics, the CFL, United Societies, and Independence League were calling it a victory for the people and independent politics. The *American* characterized the anticharter vote as a splendid example of how the machine politicians would suffer defeat when the independent voters united for reform.[7] William O'Connell, chairman of the Cook County Democratic Central Committee and Edward Dunne's ally, declared that "the men of Chicago will not accept a charter prepared for them by a convention of special interests and given its finishing touches in a legislature dominated by partisan politics."[8]

Once this initial flurry of predictable rhetoric subsided,

however, most of these same people acknowledged that this charter's defeat was not and could not be the last word on the question of municipal structural reform. The crushing administrative and fiscal problems had not vanished. Where was the city to go from here in terms of reform? The CFL and Independence League stayed on the course they had set during the charter campaign. They called again for a new charter to be written by a representative convention. It is evident that for some years after the charter's defeat they maintained their belief in a fundamental position they had staked out in the charter campaign: that the political struggle was one between the bulk of the people and the special interests of politicians, the wealthy, and the corporations. The Independence League, for example, called for the "right" charter to be drafted by a popularly elected assembly. "Such a people's convention," the league said, "would present to the legislature a bill that would speak with the voice of Chicago citizens as expressed at the polls."[9]

The CFL, following much the same reasoning, called for the fight for municipal reform to be shifted into the state arena and achieved now through a new state constitution. Shortly after the charter's defeat, the CFL adopted a resolution urging a new state constitution that would reflect the organization's understanding of the political struggle in which it was involved. Read in its entirety, the reasoning contained in this resolution makes this point explicitly.[10] "Whereas, our American system of government," began the resolution,

is based on the consent of the governed, and . . . this consent cannot be obtained except that matters pertaining to government are initiated and ratified by the citizenship of the nation, state or municipality as the case may be; and . . . the spirit of all state constitutions is that each generation should have a voice in the fundamental laws by which it is to be governed; and . . . almost a generation and one-half have passed since such a convention was held in our state owing to the manipulation of politics, in the control of PIRATICAL wealth, who continually conspire to prevent the citizenship from exercising its constitutional right to frame the fundamental law of the state; and . . .

this manipulation at times takes the form of special laws or charters for some municipalities, as against others, the intention being to array some sections of the state against others, so as to create domestic hostility, and in this way prevent united action for a common purpose; therefore, be it RESOLVED, that we most emphatically denounce such legislative conduct, and proclaim that we ask nothing for one municipality that we are not willing to grant all, and in this spirit we insist that a state constitutional convention be called as promptly as possible.

Although the CFL may have distrusted and feared the downstate politicians, it did not necessarily distrust its fellow citizens in the state. The CFL thought that if the ordinary citizens were accorded their rights to govern themselves, they would do it fairly and justly.[11]

In mid-October, the City Club scheduled another discussion on charter reform. This time, months after it should have taken better notice of the opposition to the charter, the club invited Raymond Robins and Nicholas Michels of the United Societies to address the group in the company of Charles Merriam. The theme of the discussion was the direction in which the city should go next on the question of charter reform. Robins informed his listeners that there existed little hope of any charter resembling the defeated one ever passing in the city. He predicted that no new charter would ever be accepted by the voters of Chicago unless it was popularly written and embodied the ideas about good municipal government held by the majority of Chicagoans. The people of the city, he said, "do really intend to govern Chicago. They intend to make Chicago what they want it to be, and if they don't want it to be what you want it to be your wise policy will be directed toward changing their desire and point of view." Furthermore, Robins pointed out, ultimatums from the state legislature or appeals to accept a new charter based on the rationale that it was the best Chicago could expect to get from that body were simply not acceptable to the city.[12]

With the CFL promoting a state constitutional convention and the independent forces within the city warning that any new charter had to reflect majority sentiment, the prospects for

obtaining the type of business-oriented charter desired by most
civic and business leaders did indeed seem dim. The attitude and
actions of the United Societies in the months following the referendum only reinforced this situation. In the aftermath of the
charter's defeat, it was obvious that the charter campaign had
led the leaders of the United Societies to believe that there now
existed an ongoing struggle within the city over who would control the municipal government and to what ends. Thus, the organization showed its determination to assert itself more forcefully in municipal affairs so that it might help determine the
outcome of this struggle. In the glow of victory the day after the
referendum, Nicholas Michels had proclaimed, "We have not
only won, we are preparing for a second fight."[13] He reiterated
this idea before the City Club a month later when he warned the
audience that the campaign had been a "great lesson for those
who thought they could control the city and the votes of the ethnic groups" and expressed the United Societies' position that no
new charter would ever be acceptable that did not provide for
free and equal elections, a uniform and equitable system of taxation, and home rule. "In all future charters," Michels said, "the
rights of the majority should be considered instead of the ar-
rogant demands of private interests and political bosses."[14]

To put some teeth into its rhetoric, the United Societies began to involve itself more and more in municipal affairs. At an
organizational meeting in January 1908, the United Societies
decided to move actively into the political arena, with Michels
declaring that "the results of the charter vote must be repeated.
We must promote politics—although not party politics. We must
see that liberal-minded men hold power."[15] The obvious place for
the United Societies to start its new political program was with
the next municipal elections coming in April 1908. The political
action committee of the organization, doing much as the Municipal Voters League had done a few years before, assessed all
aldermanic candidates and requested them to take a pledge.
Whereas the hallmark of the MVL had been their so-called nonpartisan pledge, the United Societies sought from the candidates
a promise to support the organization's stand against Sunday
closings, high saloon licenses, and all temperance measures in
general.[16]

The substance of the pledge had been decided at a mass gathering of the United Societies held in mid-February. At this meeting, the members passed a resolution declaring that they would "support peaceful living together and orderly society . . . hold themselves to the principle of moderation in all things and against excess, crime and sin . . . support a strong police surveillance of all taverns and meeting places . . . but believe the prohibition laws are not effective and that men are not reformed through coercive laws." Thus, the United Societies resolved, they were justified in demanding that "the obsolete blue laws be recalled and that the use of public funds to enforce these obsolete laws also cease, and that the wishes and rights of the great majority of our citizens be respected." [17] The fact that twenty-two of the thirty-five aldermen elected that April had supported the United Societies' pledge [18] gives further evidence of the high level of antiprohibition sentiment within the city and to the potential influence of the United Societies in municipal affairs, including any further attempts at charter reform. [19]

In late 1908, several of the former delegates from the 1906–7 convention did in fact decide to revive the charter movement. These men called upon their fellow delegates from the old convention to reassemble and begin their work again. In September of 1908, forty-four of these former delegates met to consider the best way to go about writing another charter. In the intervening year since the charter's defeat, a number of these men had come to accept the idea that in order to achieve any new charter they had to be prepared to make more concessions. When they met this time, they decided to draft a new charter by comparing the original as written by the convention with the version that had come out of the legislature, to take into consideration the objections that had been raised to both versions, and to attempt to arrive at "just compromises" on the disputed provisions. [20] However, no matter what compromises they might eventuate, the conspicuous hostility toward this convention on the part of the CFL did not bode well for any new charter. Although CFL member James Linehan attended several sessions of this convention, the CFL leadership steadfastly maintained that charter reform should only be undertaken by a constitutional convention. When prevailed upon to give its support to certain proposals before the charter convention, the organization announced that it "refuses to recognize the Charter Convention as having the right to draw up a charter for the city of Chicago." This assembly, said the CFL, was an "effort to deprive the people of this state of their natural and constitutional right to alter or amend the present constitution."[21]

Nonetheless, the forty-four delegates carried on with the new task they had set themselves. They quickly decided that revenue and Sunday closings were the more troublesome issues with which they had to contend. Walter Fisher now urged that a new charter contain strong home-rule provisions on liquor, taxation, and revenues.[22] Before tackling the sticky issue of liquor, the convention addressed the questions of taxation and revenue and general home-rule powers. While avoiding a strong home-rule stance, the delegates did rewrite the home-rule provision to remove the city somewhat from the control of the state legislature. They also agreed to several changes in the revenue sections. To lessen fears of higher taxes, the new version of the charter reduced the limit of allowable bonded indebtedness from 5 to 4 percent. They also replaced a vaguely worded section of the old charter with a new provision specifying that, for general tax purposes, assessed property valuation would be 1 percent of the full valuation. The new version of the charter also restored the old ward system of thirty-five wards with two aldermen each, and, to assure that the legislature could not change it again, included a provision that it could only be altered through a referendum begun by petition of 15 percent of Chicago voters.[23]

Chicago women viewed this new convention as another opportunity to demand municipal suffrage. This time the delegates reversed their earlier position and acceded to the wishes of some delegates and the Illinois Equal Suffrage Association that women be allowed to speak directly to the convention.[24] Although a number of women did appear before the convention and presented their case forcefully, the majority of delegates still did not want to include the municipal suffrage in a new charter. Charles Merriam pleaded that it should be incorporated into the charter because any separate bill would be rejected by the legislature, but his fellow delegates rejected his arguments and voted for a separate bill. Once again some of them expressed their opposition to ever giving women the vote; others, such as Walter Fisher, continued to walk a tightrope, not wishing to appear against such a liberal reform but still unwilling to commit themselves to taking the big step. Fisher suggested that the sentiment of the entire female population be polled before the laws should be changed.[25]

The appearance of women before the convention was followed quickly by that of representatives from both sides of the liquor question. Walter Michaelis of the United Societies told the delegates that his organization wanted what it had requested from the old convention: that any new charter vest the city council with sole power to regulate the sale of liquor in the city. "We want our program placed in the charter," Michaelis explained. "We are tired of submitting our plan to separate bills to the legislature."[26] The United Societies also demanded of the delegates that they insert a specific clause into the charter's provisions on liquor regulation providing "that no such general law hereafter enacted shall apply to or be operative within said city of Chicago, unless said law shall be first consented to by a majority of the legal voters of said city voting on the question."[27] Arthur Farwell, representative of the Law and Order League, knew which way the voters of Chicago would go if given the choice on liquor regulation, and he countered the United Societies' position by demanding that the charter acknowledge the state legislature's superior position on this question. "It is dangerous to give it to the council," he told the convention. "The farmers of the state are stronger on moral questions than is the council. [But] if the state were liquor and the city dry then I would want the city to control."[28] The delegates, this time, agreed with the United Societies and placed both of its desired provisions into the new charter.[29]

Whether the delegates had succeeded in framing a compromise charter that could have been supported by many of those Chicagoans who had opposed the first charter will never be known. Obviously there were still problems with the document: the consolidation scheme remained the same, as did that for the board of education, women were again furious about the lack of suffrage, and the CFL continued to believe that only a constitutional convention should undertake municipal reform. But before the public response to the new version of the charter could be tested, several of the more conservative delegates took control of the convention and destroyed any possibility of its acceptance. Led by B. E. Sunny, these men proposed that rather than submitting an entire charter scheme to the legislature, they break down their work into a number of separate bills. That way, they argued, the legislature was free to pick and choose what it wanted, without endangering the whole charter as had happened last time.[30] In despair, Walter Fisher pleaded with his fellow delegates not to undermine the proposed charter in this fashion, for he knew well by now that such an alternative was totally unacceptable to much of the city. "The charter . . . is a compromise," he told the convention. "Every provision is a compromise, and I am opposed to having those provisions made into separate bills. If we must ask for what we want and need, let us ask exactly what we should have—not compromises." But his pleas were in vain, and the delegates voted nineteen to seventeen to submit separate bills to the legislature.[31]

If Fisher despaired of the sensibilities of his fellow delegates, the United Societies was livid at this turn of events. Michaelis and Anton Cermak, who was rapidly becoming the guiding force of the United Societies, lashed out at the convention for betraying them and threatened not to support the separate bills. "We are not going to vote for a lot of measures for these so-called reformers and then get stuck ourselves," Cermak said.[32] Moreover, the bill on liquor regulation was changed before it was sent to the legislature. Unlike the original version that had declared no future state law on liquor would apply in Chicago, the amended version stated that such laws would not be presumed to cover the city if they conflicted with the liquor bill *unless* the legislature expressly declared that the law would cover the entire state.[33] This was really a gratuitous alteration. Because separate bills were being submitted to the legislature and the fate of the consolidation and revenue bills no longer had any ties to that of the liquor bill, the men responsible for the change should have been satisfied to let the United Societies have its chance at passing the bill in the form it wanted.

Once again, Chicagoans readied themselves to go to Springfield to lobby for and against charter legislation. Before the lobbying could even get underway, Mayor Busse, who had remained characteristically silent during the past several months, sealed the charter's fate. With the help of his old friend, House Speaker Shurtleff, Busse pushed through the legislature a series of new state bond laws that would have implications for the charter bills. These bond bills raised the assessed valuation factor for calculating property taxes. Simultaneously, the legislature defeated a proposed amendment that would have mandated a referendum vote on any new bond measures.[34] Chicago legislators, thenceforth, found themselves caught between the proverbial rock and the hard place: the charter consolidation bill would raise the bond limit higher than the Busse bills and thereby raise taxes higher, an anathema to many of their constituents; on the other hand, the consolidation bill contained the referendum clause that the Busse bills did not. The city was going to get one or the other piece of legislation. Business groups in Chicago, such as the Union League Club and the Chamber of Commerce, hedged their bets by supporting both measures.[35]

In the end, however, the issue was virtually taken out of the hands of Chicagoans. When the consolidation bill came to a vote, it failed in both houses of the legislature, mainly for lack of support from downstate legislators. Yet again these men attempted to trade legislation for Chicago for permanent restriction of the city's representation.[36] Having once again failed in this endeavor, they voted heavily against the consolidation bill. In the Senate, the tally was seventeen against and sixteen in favor, with all but one of the affirmative votes cast by a Chicago or Cook County legislator. Two Cook County senators did vote against the bill; one of them was Cyril Jandus, a member of the United Societies.[37] A week later, the House defeated the bill by a wide margin, this time with twenty-three Cook County representatives either voting against it or abstaining. Anton Cermak, as he had earlier said he would, voted to reject the consolidation bill.[38] The defeat of the consolidation bill took the steam out of the charter reformers. In quick order, as Walter Fisher had gloomily foreseen, the legislature rejected all of the remaining charter bills.

Chicago had another chance at charter reform in 1914. In

that year, after debating the problem for some time, the city council created a thirty-member commission and charged it with drafting a charter that would consolidate the taxing bodies and give the city government power to control public utilities and completely overhaul the revenue system.[39] The commission's work, however, was disdained by the state legislature, which only passed a bill to consolidate the parks into the municipal government. And even this bill was defeated by a city referendum vote.[40] This was the last time Chicago attempted to secure a new municipal charter separate from the rest of the state.

The story of Chicago's charter reform movement, nonetheless, cannot finish without a short description of the constitutional convention of 1920. Once it became clear that a new charter would probably never be secured from the legislature, several charter proponents adopted the idea long held by the CFL and Independence League that charter reform could be accomplished through a constitutional convention. Figuring prominently among these men was George Cole, a member of several civic organizations in the city and of all three charter sessions. Cole organized and headed a group called the Constitutional Convention League, which was dedicated to securing a new state constitution.[41] The efforts in this direction paid off in 1918 and 1919 when the voters of the state approved a constitutional convention and then elected delegates, who began their work in 1920.[42]

The possibility of potential conflicts between Chicago and the rest of the state over such a convention and its work was virtually guaranteed in the delegate selection process. The delegates were to be elected on the basis of state senatorial districts. But the state had not been redistricted since 1901, leaving Chicago and Cook County greatly underrepresented in the state legislature. Aware of this problem all along, the CFL had worked hard in 1919 to try to elect as many convention delegates favorable to its ideas as it could.[43] But, given the fact that it could do nothing about the problems of Illinois' representation scheme, there was little that labor could do to affect the absolute outcome of the voting. Thus, when the constitutional convention convened, Chicago found itself with thirty-eight representatives instead of the forty-eight it would have had if there had been true proportional representation within the state.[44]

The eventual outcome of this attempt to write a new constitution was fairly predictable in light of the regional quarrels of the past few decades. The state legislature had failed in all its previous attempts to restrict permanently Cook County's representation. Now the constitutional convention tried again. First, it ratified a provision that restricted the number of representatives in both houses. This provision also stated that once a new reapportionment based on this new scheme was completed, no county losing population would ever lose representation. Apparently this move was too blatantly prejudicial even for Illinois politics, and the convention subsequently passed a compromise provision giving proportional representation in the House and setting a fixed percentage for the number of state senators from Cook County.[45] Some Chicagoans were willing to accept this restriction scheme in return for more home rule for Chicago,[46] but others were infuriated. In addition, the constitution did not grant much home rule to municipalities. In particular, it reserved the right to impose new taxes and to set limits on the borrowing of money to the state legislature.[47] When the document was put before the voters of Illinois in December 1922, they rejected it. Chicago and Cook County opposed the new constitution overwhelmingly. Some familiar names in Chicago led the anticonstitution campaign: Edward Dunne, Harold Ickes, and Clarence Darrow, for example, had formed a group called the Peoples' Protective League to defeat the proposed constitution. Even the daily newspapers, including the *Tribune*, opposed this proposed constitution. The voters of Chicago and Cook County turned down the constitution by a margin of twenty to one. By comparison, the rest of the state voted against the constitution by a margin of two to one.

CONCLUSION

CHICAGO REMAINS UNREFORMED

The reason Chicagoans failed to agree upon and implement any type of charter reform lay deeply rooted in their past political culture. It did not lay in "reformer" versus "bosses" antagonisms or in hostility toward reform. Each side in the charter battle had different ideas about the correct priorities of municipal government. Those in favor of the charter valued strict fiscal controls over all sectors of the municipal government. The opponents of the charter, in contrast, believed that public utilities and public schools, for instance, should be conceived of as vital services provided by the city to assure and constantly improve the quality of life for all the people of the city. They ultimately turned against the 1907 charter because they believed that it would implement a municipal government dedicated to using the wrong means to achieving the wrong ends.

Yet these features of Chicago's charter reform movement have not been appreciated. There are several reasons for this. To begin with, Chicago and its municipal issues have been viewed through the lens of the business and civic "reformers." The influence of this distorted vision can be seen in the analysis of the ongoing controversy over reform of the public schools in the years surrounding the charter movement. The Chicago *Tribune* and Chicago *Daily News*, when they opposed Mayor William Hale Thompson during his first term in office (1915–19), have been referred to as "long the spokesmen for municipal reform." [1] However, to many people in the city at that time, these newspapers were big business, and as such they were the spokesmen for business, not for municipal reform. In fact, many Chicagoans sincerely believed that these same newspapers had helped thwart reform of the board of education's land leasing policy. The board of education had, in the late nineteenth century, begun a policy of leasing out many parcels of land at relatively low rates for a term to last ninety-nine years without revaluation of the property over time. Among the beneficiaries of this largesse were the *Tribune* and *Daily News*, the former having secured the land for its own building in this manner. The newspapers strenuously fought all attempts to annul these leases, disputing the contention that the rates were too low and arguing that the long-term leases were beneficial to the board of education because they guaranteed a yearly income from its properties. [2] Not everyone in the city saw it that way. The CFL was particularly incensed by "sweetheart" deals that allowed "business interests to appropriate the property of the public schools" to "further plunder school funds and . . . to commercialize the public schools in the interest of big business." [3] This was a primary reason that many people in Chicago had wanted to change from an appointive to an elective board. They objected to the schools being run by businessmen along "business lines" and thus they refused to accept the proposed charter's provisions that would have placed the public schools more squarely in the hands of businessmen.

Another reason that the charter movement has been ignored is that Chicago's political development has rarely been treated as a historical process. Because Chicago politics have seemed so interesting and exotic, ever since the early part of this century scholars have tended to write about politics—that is, political structures and political personalities—rather than politi-

cal history. This approach was fostered by the social scientists at
the University of Chicago earlier in the century who viewed the
city as a laboratory and were chiefly interested in examining
how the political party system and the political machine worked.[4]
In their work, these social scientists drew their inspiration heavily from two sources. The first source derived from the mechanisms of current politics as they appeared before their eyes; the
second source involved the writings of those of their number
who had been active in Chicago politics at one time or another.
Chief among them was, of course, Charles Merriam.

This concentration on current politics and the excessive reliance on the works of people involved in one side of the political
process has resulted in a self-perpetuating cycle in which Chicago's twentieth-century municipal development has been studied in terms of politics, rather than as political history, with an
emphasis on politicians and political personalities.[5] In such an
analytical framework, politics is seen either as a game played
out among politicians—a game that has little to do with the history of the city or with the people, who are seen as interested
only in assuring their small piece of the pie—or else politicians
and their plans become a metaphor for the city as a whole in
which what the politicians want and why is assumed to be syn-
onymous with what the people themselves want and for the
same reasons. But by viewing Chicago's political history in
these ways, the impact of the charter movement on subsequent
political development has been ignored. The legacies of the ideas
sharpened during the charter campaign and of the failure to restructure the municipal government affected Chicago long after
the charter's death. The charter movement provided the context
for the development—but not yet the institutionalization—of
fledgling coalitions formed among the city's residents based on
some shared ideas about the shape and purposes of the municipal government. Among the important elements of the coalition
that would support the building of a city-wide political machine
in the following decades were, of course, the city's ethnic groups
and working class. A new evaluation of the ideas expressed by
the United Societies and the CFL during the charter reform
movement can help illuminate their reasons for participating in
the later political machine.

In assessing the United Societies, one must not confound the goals and ideas of the early founders and supporters of the organization with those of Anton Cermak, who came to control the organization in its later years. If Cermak had in mind using the United Societies as a vehicle for establishing a power base for his own political aspirations,[6] this was the action and reasoning of a politician. It does not follow ipso facto that the people who belonged to the United Societies, including the original leaders, were seeking to carve for themselves a position of power in a political party system in which only party or personality politics counted. Such an analysis removes politics from the historical context of the city. The origins of the United Societies are inextricably bound to the political culture of Chicago in the early 1900s, in the differing perceptions of good municipal government that were developing at the turn of the century, and in the constant awareness of the struggle between city and state and among people in the city for control of that government.

If one looks at the United Societies in the early 1900s, it is not accurate to characterize it as a one-issue organization. The desire to avoid prohibition was certainly foremost on the organization's agenda, but it was part of an agenda for reshaping the whole city. Thus the United Societies' antiprohibition stance was more complicated and forward-looking than the ethnocultural explanation of "personal liberty" would have it. The analysis that "the United Societies joined with CFL and the Democratic Party in opposing charter reform because ritualistic religious and ethnic groups equated the adoption of the charter with a 'return to the Puritanical Sunday'"[7] contains three assertions, only the first of which is correct. The United Societies did believe, quite accurately, that the new charter would have greatly facilitated the imposition of municipal prohibition, despite the widespread opposition within the city to such a measure. However, this was not the only reason the members of the United Societies had to oppose the charter. They opposed it because they understood that the charter in general, and the prohibition laws it might have effected in particular, would have reshaped the entire urban environment in an excessively probusiness and upper-income manner.

Furthermore, the CFL's opposition to prohibition both during the charter campaign and in the following years provides additional evidence for the connection between this issue and other urban reform issues. In 1910, the CFL argued that prohibition would result in unemployment for thousands of workers. Labor's position was more complicated than the simple argument of maintaining jobs just for the sake of jobs. The CFL pointed out the unfairness and the lack of social awareness involved in taking jobs away from people whose chances of finding other work in an already saturated labor market were minimal. But it is even more significant for underscoring the point that the CFL understood the interrelationship of urban issues that the organization criticized the prohibitionists for concentrating on the evils of liquor while ignoring the other social evils of the freewheeling capitalist system that so many of them advocated. Not only would those people thrown out of jobs be unable to find work, said the CFL, they would also receive little consideration for their plight from the rest of the non-working-class population.

Thus, the labor movement urged Chicagoans to vote against a prohibition proposition to be put before them, asking why laboring people should vote many of their own out of work, when the same "reformers" who supported prohibition were refusing to support laws that would make the jobs of so many other workers safer, healthier, and more secure. Why, labor asked, could "among all the forces arrayed on behalf of prohibition . . . the forces of organized labor find none which have cast their lot with them in the humane fight they have put up for improved conditions in the industrial world."[8] Laboring people in Chicago (and it is safe to assume that the majority of these people were "ethnics") did not see prohibition either as a reform, or solely as an issue of personal liberty. Rather, for them, it was yet another instance of businessmen and "reformers" trying to create an urban environment congenial to and protective of their own desires. "Drunkenness is a crying evil, a crime, if you will," declared the *Union Labor Advocate*. "But only a little of the effort now being put forth to bring about prohibition, if applied to an effort to bring about justice to the toiling women, children and men of Chicago and Illinois, would go far toward removing one of the greatest incentives to intemperance."[9]

In the first decade of the twentieth century, these compatible ideas about urban reform were by no means ready to be shaped into the political machine. During the charter movement, Chicagoans certainly showed no love for either party or its politicians. All suggestions to form actual political coalitions among the groups opposing the charter in 1907, especially suggestions that they align themselves with the Democratic party, were turned aside by one group or another and Chicagoans continued to spurn such moves through the next two decades. Organized labor, for example, gave its allegiance to neither party. Its vote split in the 1911 mayoral election between Carter Harrison and Charles Merriam.[10] Eight years later, the CFL founded a Labor party and ran its own candidate.[11] Labor was still split in 1931 when it was uncertain that it wished to support Anton Cermak.[12] If the politicians of the Democratic party were working out some scheme to control the political system, organized labor was still not cooperating wholeheartedly in this scheme by 1931.

What then was happening in the years between 1907 and 1931 that resulted in the building of the machine and how did the charter movement contribute to it? Recent work on contemporary Chicago politics theorizes that the political machine developed in Chicago because it was a way for Democratic politicians and their ethnic constituencies to assure control of election results.[13] This has become the shared credo of almost everyone studying Chicago's political development. The history of the charter movement suggests, on the contrary, that neither the machinations of clever politicians nor the inability of ethnic voters to break out of a traditional cultural background produced the political machine. In the first place, one needs to ask what, in terms of the political parties, were the alternatives facing Chicago voters by 1931? Charles Merriam's defeat in the 1911 mayoral election virtually finished the liberal wing of the Republican party in Chicago politics, not the least because so many of its leaders left the city, but also because they continued to promote the kind of political program for the city that too many of the voters had already rejected. Otherwise, all the party had offered Chicago was William Hale Thompson, and, by 1931, Republican businessmen and civic organizers were disgusted with him and backing Cermak.[14]

But well beyond the confines of the successes or failures of the traditional party system, the development of Chicago's "peculiar" political institutions grew from the historical circumstances of the charter reform movement. Chicago never did secure a new municipal charter under which to govern itself in the twentieth century. Nor did the city ever achieve much meaningful home-rule power. It was not until 1970 that the people of Illinois wrote and adopted a new constitution somewhat altering the state laws regarding municipalities. This new constitution does confer some measure of home rule on Illinois cities, but in reality these home-rule powers, especially the very important powers of taxation and revenue, remain quite restricted. Thus Chicago has never managed to free itself legally from its constricting and often prejudical ties to the state legislature.

Moreover, without actual structural consolidation and centralization, Chicago became increasingly ungovernable in the years following the charter's defeat because there was no structural means to impose order and centralized decision making on the municipal government. Few people involved in the charter fight had rejected centralized government as a concept. The crucial distinction instead had been how to accomplish centralization and how to delegate and exercise power and authority within this new structure. Without centralization, Chicago retained the separate governing and taxing authorities and could not localize power within the municipality. The city also retained its strong-council system, wherein the ability of the mayor to function often depended on whatever support he could muster in the council. Such a system has favored a strong personality—such as that of William Hale Thompson, a two-term mayor from 1915–23 who served a third term in 1927–31—a person whose personality could overpower the political will of any opposition in the Council.

But even the continuance of the strong-council system did not have to prove totally detrimental for the city: if the council could have had control over more of the municipal decision making, then it would have been the locus of power. As it was, however, this was impossible. How could a coherent ongoing policy toward, for, say, the school system be instituted when the mayor appointed but could not remove board members; when the council could thwart but not propose or implement school budgets or policies; when the citizens were expected to send their children to the schools, but given virtually no say in the system? Where is the locus of power in such a situation? Who makes the decisions and has the power to implement them?

The political machine ultimately provided a way around this otherwise ungovernable structural mess left by the failure of charter reform. The machine brought centralized government to Chicago: it found a way to implement the control over the entire municipal government system that had not been accomplished by the structural reform of overlapping authorities or attained through the institution of home rule. By controlling both the machinery of the municipal government, in the offices of the mayor and aldermen, and the county-wide Democratic party system, the Democratic political machine ultimately imposed de facto centralized order on a de jure decentralized system.

The examples of how Chicago's parks and public schools were run by the machine provide further illustration. Structurally, the entire municipal park system has remained a separate governing authority outside of the actual control of the city government. Under this circumstance, only by appointing people to run the parks who could be counted on to carry out the programs coming from the central office—that of the mayor—could the city exercise decision-making powers over the park system. The same was true of the public school system. When Richard Daley was mayor, for example, on more than one occasion he averted a teachers' strike by forcing an agreement between the board of education and the teachers' union. The mayor had no legitimate authority to do this; he had no authority to sit in on the negotiations, propose the terms of settlement, or force anyone involved to accept his proposals. Yet he succeeded because the people on the board were his people, and both sides in the negotiations believed that he had the power to carry out whatever he promised in the bargain, be it finding more money for the schools or giving his tacit support to the union. Only with the assured acquiescence and loyalty of all the people involved in running the park and school systems could the city's lack of legal structural control over these vital municipal services be surmounted.

The relationship between the mayor and the city council similarly illustrates how the machine imposed centralized authority on the city. Technically, Chicago remains a strong-council government in which the aldermen hold the power to thwart any proposals, budgets, or programs emanating from the mayor's office. But when Daley was mayor, it looked to all the world as if Chicago had a strong mayor form of government because he always got what he wanted. He was able to do so only because all the people involved chose to acquiesce to his desires or perhaps were given good reasons to acquiesce, but not because Daley had the legal power to make them comply.

The fact is that the political machine gave too many Chicagoans what they wanted for them to reject it. If the business community and civic reformers had supported Cermak in 1931 because they could no longer stomach the ravings of the Republican candidate, in the following years they found other reasons for supporting the machine. The municipal order it gradually instituted became a true asset for doing business in the city. This was especially true during the Daley years: although various business leaders gave lip service to being antimachine, in reality they understood that the orderly political climate that Daley fostered in the city favored business.

On the other hand, although the people who had first united against the 1907 charter were in 1931 not yet securely in the Democratic coalition or under Cermak's sway, they had by then considerable experience at working together and with the Democrats. It was not long before the benefits of the new order became apparent to them. As the agent of centralizing the municipal government, the machine finally gave to the people of Chicago a way, at least for a while, to control and shape the city in the ways they had expressed during the charter campaign. If the legal structure did not give them an elective school board, for example, the machine gave them the belief, and to some extent the reality, that they had more control over the schools because they were directly a part of the political system that would choose the board of education. Just as the businessmen reformers of the early part of the century had wanted to restructure the municipal government to put themselves in control of the city, the political machine for decades gave the people of Chicago a feeling that they were in control, that what they wanted mattered and would be listened to. The labor and ethnic coalition loosely formed earlier in the century was consolidated and institutionalized into the backbone of the machine because this political system ordered the city in the ways these people desired.

The role of the machine in making effective a system of government that was otherwise ungovernable has become more apparent in contemporary Chicago as the Machine has ceased to function well. Until mid-1986, Mayor Harold Washington enjoyed only minority support among the aldermen and the tacit coalition between his office and the council that had allowed previous mayors to look strong was ruptured. The majority was able constantly to thwart or stall his proposals. This impasse was not broken until a ward redistricting mandated that new elections be held and the results secured an aldermanic majority for the mayor.

Furthermore, Chicago still has a nineteenth-century type of municipal government. When charter reform failed, it left intact the cumbersome, decentralized structure of overlapping governing and taxing authorities. Only the three park districts were consolidated into one district in 1934 under the authority conferred by the enabling amendment of 1904. Yet this provided small relief to the problem of overlapping municipal authorities. The park district, the county government, the sanitary district, and the board of education remain as separate agencies operating within the city but for the most part little subject to legal control by the municipal government. In the meantime, additional separate authorities have been created to complicate further Chicago's municipal life. There is now a forest-preserve district and a junior-college district.[15] The Chicago Transit Authority and Regional Transit Authority are autonomous bodies created by state laws. And for the past few years, a state-created fiscal control board has overseen the administration of the school system.

All of this means that legally and structurally Chicago still has no secure control over important aspects of municipal life. The county government still controls the assessment of property. It also administers the few public hospitals and the public welfare system. It is possible to argue that this latter situation saves the municipal government from the expenses involved in financing the public hospitals and welfare systems. As a shrewd politician, Daley exploited this situation to the maximum financial benefit of the city. On the other hand, it means that the city has no control over two public services extremely vital to the welfare of its citizens; after all, the people of Chicago are primarily the ones who need these services and not the residents of the increasingly wealthier suburbs of Cook County. There is, in fact, a deplorable lack of public health facilities in Chicago compared with, for example, New York City, which has an extensive network of public hospitals. Unfortunately, this situation will not be bettered in the future as the people of the county become less inclined to support public welfare programs and as their numbers increase while those of the city decrease.

Because it lacked legal and structural control of municipal services the machine could never institutionalize the idea of the opponents of the 1907 charter that the highest priorities of a municipal government should be to protect and further the social welfare of the majority of the citizens. The appalling lack of public-health services is but one example of this failure. The public transit system is another. After the defeat of the municipal ownership drives in the early part of the century, Chicago never came close to having anything resembling true municipal ownership and operation of public utilities. The creation, in 1913, of a state commission to regulate public utilities and franchises—a type of regulatory agency favored by many businessmen "reformers"—kept control of the transit system away from the city. Not until after World War II did the creation of the Chicago Transit Authority finally remove public transit from private ownership. The CTA is an agency created by state law, subject to municipal ordinances but still outside much control by the city government.

By allowing the public transit system to remain in private ownership for so long, Chicago has never solved the problems generated by that system. Certain areas of the city remain drastically underserviced, for example, and the older el lines are badly deteriorated for want of sustained attention throughout the century, a fault that is now compounded by the huge deficits of the CTA. Without municipal ownership, no one in Chicago has ever developed the perspective toward public utilities that the advocates of municipal ownership had tried to instill earlier in the century: that is, the belief that public transit and indeed all public utilities are vital municipal services that must be adequately funded, carefully maintained, and well run in order to assure the quality of life in a city.

Still another example of the shortcomings of the machine is the fact that it could never secure legal control of the school system for the city. The board of education is still appointed, but once in place it has little accountability to the public. Moreover, the system suffers now more than ever before from being at the mercy of the state legislature. On the one hand, the state requires that the Chicago public schools have a balanced budget; on the other hand, state legislators and the governor chronically underfund the system, even to the extent of arrogantly refusing to obey the state laws in this regard. Because the city thus has so little control over the revenues for funding education, the school system has grown increasingly poorer. Its physical plants deteriorate, the middle class abandon the system, leaving it a constituency poorer and in need of more help, and the state government remains hostile to the city's needs. When, as a result of the severe fiscal crisis of the schools in the late 1970s, the state created a fiscal control board to oversee all Chicago school expenditures, the city's helplessness was further exposed. The person placed in charge of this board was not even a Chicagoan, and the board's mandate to insure the implementation of a balanced budget provoked a teachers' strike in each of the school years of 1983, 1984, and 1985. The mandate for a balanced budget clashed with the desires of the teachers for pay raises and a continuation of their pension and benefit funds. In none of these strike situations was the municipal government able to intervene and attempt to mediate the strikes or to prevent them from occurring in the first place.

Indeed one of the most striking points about Chicago's schools—and about every other aspect of municipal government—is the way the issues raised in the early 1900s, not having been resolved then, remain problems today. In 1907, at the charter convention, Louis Post had denounced the "midnight sessions of [the board of education] when public property was voted away to the value of millions of dollars . . . and we, gentlemen, are hoping to get back a lot of that plunder that the business men . . . were paid to take away from the school children."[16] The very same arguments can be heard today in Chicago. In early 1980, for instance, a group calling itself Citizens for a Better Chicago vehemently protested the probability of a new school board packed with businessmen (a result of the current financial crisis and the appointment of the fiscal oversight board) and called for a board of education composed of educators and parents who would not lose sight of the children and the purposes of education.[17]

Neither in 1907 during the charter campaign nor now are disagreements over the school system primarily a question of personalities or party politics. Chicagoans hold different ideas about public schools. They also disagree about the nature of the urban environment and about good municipal government. On the basis of their ideas, people in Chicago adopted their positions on charter reform in 1907 and they have continued to do so on municipal issues since that time.

NOTES

BIBLIOGRAPHY

INDEX

NOTES

Introduction

1. The literature on charter reform is extensive. The best overviews on the subject are Charles Beard, *American City Government: A Survey of Newer Tendencies* (New York: Century, 1912); Ernest Griffith, *A History of American City Government: The Conspicuous Failure, 1870–1900* and *A History of American City Government: The Progressive Years, 1900–1920* (New York: Praeger, 1974); and Martin Schiesl, *The Politics of Efficiency: Municipal Administration and Reform in America, 1880–1920* (Berkeley: University of California, 1977).

2. Illinois, Constitution (1870), article 4, section 22. For the early history of Chicago's municipal government see Hugo Grosser, *Chicago: A Review of Its Governmental History, 1837–1906* (Chicago, 1906), and Samuel E. Sparling, *Municipal History and Present Organization of the City of Chicago* (Madison, 1898).

3. Joseph M. Bessette and Jeffrey Tulis, "The Constitution, Politics, and the Presidency," in *The Presidency in the Constitutional Order*, ed. Joseph M. Bessette and Jeffrey Tulis (Baton Rouge: Louisiana State University, 1981).

4. See the essays in Michael Ebner and Eugene Tobin, eds., *The Age of Urban Reform: New Perspectives on the Progressive Era* (Port Washington: Kennikat, 1977).

5. To explain why Chicago developed a political machine while New York did not, for example, one study attributed political development to the impersonal forces and circumstances of geography. "Clearly New York's circular shape, which permitted the development of middle-class neighborhoods in several directions . . . is an important factor in that city's political history, as is the narrow waist of Chicago and Philadelphia, or Detroit's short northeast corridor." But to make the theory fit, these cities had to be seen as alike in other aspects of their political development. Thus, Chicago was said to have experienced "the wave of

structural reform that swept the country," just as New York did. Chicago did undertake some reforms, but it never restructured its municipal government. That is a critical structural and political difference between the two cities. Michael McCarthy, "On Bosses, Reformers, and Urban Growth: Some Suggestions for a Political Typology of American Cities," *Journal of Urban History* 4 (November 1977): 30, 33. See also McCarthy, "Businessmen and Professionals in Municipal Reform: The Chicago Experience, 1887–1920" (Ph.D. Diss., Northwestern University, 1970).

6. David B. Truman, *The Governmental Process: Political Interests and Public Opinion* (New York: Alfred Knopf, 1971).

7. See for example Richard M. Bernard and Bradley R. Rice, "Political Environment and the Adoption of Progressive Municipal Reform," *Journal of Urban History* 2 (February 1975): 149–74; John Buenker, *Urban Liberalism and Progressive Reform* (New York: Norton, 1973); Carl V. Harris, *Political Power in Birmingham, 1871–1921* (Knoxville: University of Tennessee, 1977); Samuel Hays, "The Politics of Reform in Municipal Government in the Progressive Era," *Pacific Northwest Quarterly* 55 (October 1964): 157–69; Ira Katznelson, *City Trenches: Urban Politics and the Patterning of Class in the U.S.* (New York: 1981); McCarthy, "On Bosses, Reformers, and Urban Growth"; and Schiesl, *The Politics of Efficiency.*

8. Paul Kleppner, *The Cross of Culture: A Social Analysis of Midwestern Politics, 1850–1900* (New York: The Free Press, 1970), pp. 169, 178. For Chicago specifically see also John Buenker, "The Dynamics of Chicago Ethnic Politics, 1900–1930," *Journal of the Illinois State Historical Society* 67 (April 1974), and Joel Tarr, *A Study in Boss Politics: William Lorimer of Chicago* (Urbana: University of Illinois, 1971). Also, Paul Kleppner, *Chicago Divided: The Making of a Black Mayor* (DeKalb: Northern Illinois University Press, 1985), especially chapter 2.

9. That urban ethnic groups may have had a different vision of city life and urban governments is suggested by John Buenker in his book on urban liberalism, but the theoretical apparatus of ethnoculturism overwhelms this. See Buenker, *Urban Liberalism and Progressive Reform.*

10. Kathleen Neils Conzen, "Quantification and the New Urban History," *Journal of Interdisciplinary History* (Spring 1983): 658–59.

11. See for example, Samuel Hays, "The Changing Political Structure of the City in Industrial America," *Journal of Urban History* 1 (November 1974): 6–38.

12. See Kathleen McCarthy, *Noblesse Oblige: Charity and Cultural*

Philanthropy in Chicago, 1849–1929 (Chicago: University of Chicago, 1982), for an example of the lost community theory as applied to the development of the idea of public welfare in Chicago.

13. David Nord, "The Public Community: The Urbanization of Journalism in Chicago," *Journal of Urban History* 11 (August 1985): 412, 416, 436–37.

14. Ibid., 429–30.

15. Schiesl, *The Politics of Efficiency*, p. 192.

1. City of Progress, City of Problems

1. For these and other impressions of Chicago in 1893 see Paul M. Angle, ed., *Prairie State: Impressions of Illinois, 1673–1967* (Chicago: University of Chicago, 1968), and Bessie L. Pierce, *As Others See Chicago: Impressions of Visitors, 1673–1933* (Chicago: University of Chicago, 1933).

2. For general accounts of Chicago's economic development in this period, see Bessie L. Pierce, *History of Chicago*, vol. 3, *The Rise of the Modern City, 1871–1893* (Chicago: University of Chicago, 1957), Harold M. Mayer and Richard O. Wade, *Chicago: Growth of a Metropolis* (Chicago: University of Chicago, 1969), and Charles Merriam, *Chicago: A More Intimate View of Urban Politics* (New York: Macmillan, 1929).

3. Paul Barrett, *The Automobile and Urban Transit: The Formation of Public Policy in Chicago, 1900–1930* (Philadelphia: Temple University Press, 1983), p. 15.

4. City of Chicago Department of Development and Planning, *Historic City: The Settlement of Chicago* (Chicago: 1976), p. 43.

5. The best accounts of the annexation movement are in Michael McCarthy, "Businessmen and Professionals in Municipal Reform: The Chicago Experience, 1887–1920" (Ph.D. Diss., Northwestern University, 1970), pp. 1–21; Bessie Pierce, *History of Chicago*, vol. 3, pp. 331–33; and Mayer and Wade, *Growth of a Metropolis*, pp. 154–78.

6. Angle, *Prairie State*, p. 426; Pierce, *As Others See Chicago*, pp. 251, 276–77.

7. Angle, *Prairie State*, p. 426.

8. Chicago Department of Health, *Biennial Report* (1895–1896), pp. 63–64; Robert Hunter, *Tenement Conditions in Chicago: A Report by the Investigating Committee of the City Homes Association* (Chicago: City Homes Association, 1901), passim. See also Jane Addams, *Twenty Years at Hull-House* (New York: Macmillan, 1910); and Thomas Lee Philpott, *The Slum and the Ghetto: Neighborhood Deterioration and Middle-Class Reform, Chicago, 1880–1930* (New York: Oxford, 1978).

9. See Addams, *Twenty Years at Hull-House*, pp. 200–211, for her description of these conditions in the Hull House neighborhood on Chicago's near west side.

10. Angle, *Prairie State*, p. 431.

11. Howard Chudacoff, *The Evolution of American Urban Society* (Englewood Cliffs, NJ: Prentice-Hall, 1975), p. 91. In Chicago, 77.5 percent of the population was foreign stock, while in New York and Milwaukee it was 78.6 percent; Chicago's foreign-born population was 35.7 percent compared with 40.4 percent for New York and 35.9 percent for Boston.

12. Lincoln Steffens, *The Shame of the Cities* (New York: McClure, 1902) provides a contemporary account of municipal franchise corruption. Barrett, *The Automobile and Urban Transit*, Ray Ginger, *Altgeld's America* (New York: New Viewpoints, 1973), and Melvin Holli, *Reform in Detroit: Hazen S. Pingree and Urban Politics* (New York: Oxford, 1969), assess the franchise question in Chicago and Detroit.

13. Nick A. Komons, "Chicago, 1893–1907: The Politics of Reform" (Ph.D. Diss., George Washington University, 1961), pp. 123, 135.

14. Hoyt King, "The Reform Movement in Chicago," *The Annals* 25 (March 1905): 235.

15. Norma Evenson, *Paris, A Century of Change: 1878–1978* (New Haven: Yale University Press, 1979), pp. 76–77.

16. See James Weinstein, "Organized Business and the City Commission and Manager Movements," *Journal of Southern History* 28 (1962): 166–82.

17. Charles Merriam, *Report of an Investigation of the Municipal Revenues of Chicago* (Chicago: City Club of Chicago, 1906), provides a thorough discussion of the revenue system and its shortcomings.

18. The Revenue Law of 1898 fixed a ratio of one-fifth between the assessed and the real value of property; therefore, the tax limit of Cook County was 1 percent of the total real property value.

19. Recent works on transit in Chicago have raised the question of whether Yerkes actually said this. It has become a stock quote in the lore of public transit and municipal corruption, and the fact remains that the city had little legal means to force Yerkes to change his practices. See Paul Barrett, *The Automobile and Urban Transit*, p. 18.

20. For an overview of the problems of the franchise system in late nineteenth-century Chicago see Barrett, *The Automobile and Urban Transit*; Ray Ginger, *Altgeld's America*; Carter Harrison, *Stormy Years: The Autobiography of Carter H. Harrison, Five Times Mayor of Chicago* (Indianapolis: Bobbs-Merrill, 1935); Komons, "Chicago, 1893–1907:

The Politics of Reform"; and Lloyd Wendt and Herman Kogan, *Bosses in Lusty Chicago* (Bloomington: University of Indiana, 1943).

21. The lack of communication between Chicago and the state, and the bitterness between them, could be seen as early as 1839 when the Illinois legislature in Springfield abolished the office of high constable for Chicago and notified the city only two months later, at which point Chicagoans sarcastically suggested that they be informed more quickly when the legislature decided "to remove Chicago from the shore of Lake Michigan." Quoted in Albert Lepawsky, *Home Rule for Metropolitan Chicago* (Chicago: University of Chicago, 1932), p. 114.

22. Today that is still the case. Chicago's population may have dipped slightly under three million according to the 1980 census; nevertheless, its nearest rivals do not exceed two hundred thousand. As such, Chicago, for more than a century, has been the frequent target of all rural or small town hostilities in the state toward big cities.

23. Adna F. Weber, *The Growth of Cities in the Nineteenth Century: A Study in Statistics* (New York: Macmillan, 1899; reprint edition, New York: Cornell, 1967), pp. 211, 306; William B. Philip, "Chicago and the Downstate: A Study of Their Conflicts, 1870–1934" (Ph.D. Diss., University of Chicago, 1940), pp. 2, 50.

24. Philip, pp. 16–17.

25. Ibid., pp. 36–41 and 51–54. The Senate vote to restrict representation in 1901 just failed to receive the necessary two-thirds vote, thirty-four yes to twelve no. Only one of the no votes came from outside of Cook County.

26. Paul Avrich, *The Haymarket Tragedy* (Princeton: Princeton University, 1984), p. 176.

27. Ginger, *Altgeld's America*, p. 41.

28. Avrich, *Haymarket*, pp. 186–87.

29. Ginger, *Altgeld's America*, pp. 41–42.

30. Ibid., pp. 41, 43, and Avrich, *Haymarket*, p. 97.

31. Henry David, *The History of the Haymarket Affair* (New York: Farrar and Rinehart, 1936), p. 186.

32. Avrich, *Haymarket*, pp. 184, 186.

33. Piecing together all surviving evidence, Paul Avrich has come to several conclusions about the incident. He believes that only one policeman was actually killed by the bomb; the rest died from bullet wounds (or a combination of bullet wounds and bomb wounds) inflicted upon them by their fellow officers. All of the civilian casualties were also the victims of police bullets. He also concludes that the police were virtually unrestrained in their actions: Police Lieutenant James Bowler

was heard to shout to his men "Fire and kill all you can!" and evidence also exists that Inspector Bonfield had planned to cause trouble at the meeting. See Avrich, *Haymarket*, pp. 206, 208–9, 211–13.

34. Pierce, *History of Chicago*, vol. 3, p. 281. A group of three hundred, incuding Field, Armour, and Pullman, pledged over $100,000 to help the police stamp out anarchy and sedition and a comparable sum was raised every year until 1891. See Avrich, *Haymarket*, p. 223.

35. See Ginger, *Altgeld's America*, pp. 42, 49.

36. Avrich, *Haymarket*, p. 233.

37. One of the consequences of Haymarket was passage of the state Merritt Conspiracy Bill that made liable for punishment any person who had conspired to perform an act of force or violence dangerous to human life or whose publicly spoken or written word was an incitement to an unlawful act; the bill made it unnecessary to have proof that those on trial had even come together or had made an agreement. See Pierce, *History of Chicago*, vol. 3, p. 289. The law was repealed in 1891.

38. Stanley Buder, *Pullman: An Experiment in Industrial Order and Community Planning, 1880–1930* (New York: Oxford, 1967), pp. 183–85.

39. McCarthy, "Businessmen and Professionals," p. 17.

40. See John Clayton, "The Scourge of Sinners: Arthur Burrage Farwell," *Chicago History* (Fall 1974): 68–77.

41. Chicago *Record-Herald*, February 3, February 6, and March 6, 1906.

42. *Abendpost*, March 26, 1906.

43. Ibid., May 26, 1906.

44. Jane Addams, *Twenty Years at Hull-House*, p. 122; Ginger, *Altgeld's America*, pp. 250–51.

45. Addams, *Twenty Years at Hull-House*, pp. 122–23.

46. Buder, *Pullman*, pp. 171–72.

47. King, "The Reform Movement in Chicago," p. 239.

48. For the best description of the MVL and its campaigns see Michael McCarthy, "Businessmen and Professionals in Municipal Reform: the Chicago Experience, 1887–1920"; and McCarthy, "The New Metropolis: Chicago, The Annexation Movement, and Progressive Reform," in *The Age of Urban Reform: New Perspectives on the Progressive Era*, ed. Michael Ebner and Eugene Tobin (Port Washington: Kennikat, 1977), pp. 43–54.

49. Letter of Walter L. Fisher to Marx and Door, November 16, 1903. Walter L. Fisher Papers, Library of Congress, Washington, D.C.

50. Samuel Hays, "The Politics of Urban Reform in Municipal Gov-

ernment in the Progressive Era," *Pacific Northwest Quarterly* 55 (October 1964): 161. Whether the exact term used is cosmopolitan or metropolitan, the concept is the same. See also Harold L. Platt, "City-Building and Progressive Reform: The Modernization of an Urban Polity, Houston, 1892–1905," in *The Age of Urban Reform*; and Martin Schiesl, *The Politics of Efficiency: Municipal Administration and Reform in America, 1880–1920* (Berkeley: University of California, 1977).

51. Kathleen McCarthy, *Noblesse Oblige: Charity and Cultural Philanthropy in Chicago, 1849–1929* (Chicago: University of Chicago, 1982), pp. 47–49.

52. Adade Wheeler and Marlene Wortman, *The Roads They Made: Women in Illinois History* (Chicago: Charles Kerr, 1977), pp. 63–64, 85.

53. Addams, *Twenty Years at Hull-House*, pp. 203–5.

54. Ibid., p. 100.

55. Louise DeKoven Bowen, *Growing up with a City* (New York: Macmillan, 1926), pp. 64–65.

56. Addams, p. 230; Wheeler and Wortman, *The Roads They Made*, pp. 86–87; Margaret Haley, "My Story," unpublished autobiography in Chicago Federation of Teachers Papers, boxes 32 and 33, Chicago Historical Society, Chicago, Illinois.

57. Wheeler and Wortman, pp. 87–89. The CFT continued throughout the Progressive Era to involve itself in municipal affairs that extended beyond the province of the schools.

58. Wheeler and Wortman, *The Roads They Made*, pp. 108–9, describes this impetus behind the founding in 1910 of the Woman's City Club; Bowen, *Growing Up with a City*, pp. 173–74, explains the drawing up by this organization of a Woman's Municipal Platform.

59. Addams, *Twenty Years at Hull-House*, pp. 237–38.

60. Carter Harrison, *Stormy Years*, pp. 140, 174–75.

61. Chicago *Tribune*, March 26, 1899.

62. Komons, "Chicago, 1893–1907: The Politics of Reform," pp. 296, 311–12, 319.

63. Chicago *Daily News, Almanac*, 1905, p. 357. Public-policy votes were nonbinding.

64. Ibid., 1906, p. 292. In this public-policy vote, the voters rejected the traction ordinance 150,785 to 64,391.

65. For discussion of European mass transit and the municipalization movement, see John P. McKay, *Tramways and Trolleys: The Rise of Urban Mass Transport in Europe* (Princeton: Princeton University Press, 1976), pp. 171–91.

66. Louis F. Post, "Living a Long Life Over," unpublished autobiog-

raphy in Louis F. Post Papers, box 4, Library of Congress, Washington D.C., pp. 270–72.

67. Joel A. Tarr, "William Kent to Lincoln Steffens: The Origins of Progressive Reform in Chicago," *Mid-America* 47 (January 1965): 50–51.

68. Barry J. Kaplan, "Metropolitics, Administrative Reform, and Political Theory: The Greater New York City Charter of 1897," *Journal of Urban History* 9 (February 1983): 165–94. For accounts of charter reform movements in other cities, see also Samuel Hays, "The Politics of Reform;" Richard G. Miller, "Fort Worth and the Progressive Era: The Movement for Charter Revision, 1899–1907," in *Essays on Urban America*, ed. Margaret F. Morris and Elliott West (Austin: University of Texas Press, 1975), pp. 89–126; Harold L. Platt, *City Building in the New South: The Growth of Public Services in Houston, Texas, 1830–1910* (Philadelphia: Temple University Press, 1983); and Schiesl, *The Politics of Efficiency.*

2. The Beginnings of Charter Reform

1. Chicago *Tribune*, May 4, 1897. For the arguments on home rule at the time see also Ellis P. Oberholtzer, "Home Rule for Our American Cities," *The Annals* 3 (1892–93): 736–63.

2. Chicago, *Journal of the Proceedings of the City Council*, meeting of October 14, 1901, pp. 910–11.

3. Ibid., meeting of September 29, 1902, p. 1104.

4. Chicago Civic Federation, "Preliminary Report on the Need for a New City Charter," Chicago Civic Federation Papers, box no. 3, Chicago Historical Society.

5. *Tribune*, October 28, 1902; Chicago New Charter Convention, list of delegates, in Civic Federation Papers, box no. 3.

6. Ibid.

7. Ibid.

8. *Tribune*, October 28, 1902.

9. New Charter Convention, *Proceedings*, November 25, 1902.

10. New Charter Convention, *Proceedings*, December 18, 1902, and January 7, 1903.

11. Ibid.

12. William B. Philip, "Chicago and the Downstate: A Study of Their Conflicts, 1870–1934" (Ph.D. Diss., University of Chicago, 1940), pp. 170–72; Chicago *Record-Herald*, April 23, 1903.

13. Illinois, House *Journal*, March 24, 1903, p. 386, and April 22, 1903, pp. 793, 795. The amendment became article 4, section 34, of the Illinois Constitution (1870).

14. Chicago, *Journal of the Proceedings of the City Council*, January 25, 1904, pp. 2111–12, and February 1, 1904, p. 2125; and Chicago New Charter Movement, *Why the Pending Constitutional Amendment Should Be Adopted* (1904), pamphlet, Chicago Historical Society.

15. Chicago Federation of Labor, *Minutes*, October 16, 1904, and November 4, 1904.

16. *Tribune*, November 8, 1904.

17. CFL, *Minutes*, November 4, 1904; *The Public*, November 5, 1904. *The Public* was Post's newspaper.

18. *Daily News, Almanac* (1905), p. 356.

19. *Record-Herald*, November 24, 1904.

20. Ibid.; list of delegates, in Civic Federation Papers; Albert N. Marquis, ed., *The Book of Chicagoans: A Biographical Dictionary of Leading Living Men of the City of Chicago* (Chicago: A. N. Marquis and Company, 1905 and 1911).

21. Merritt Starr to B. E. Sunny, April 14, 1904, Civic Federation Papers, box no. 3. The Union League Club, according to its historian, "numbered a large portion of Chicago's most distinguished citizens in its membership. Bankers, merchants, capitalists, railroad managers, and officers of great corporations—the 'solid men.'" Bruce Grant, *Fight for a City: The Story of the Union League Club of Chicago and Its Times, 1880–1955* (Chicago: Union League Club, 1955), p. 175.

22. CFL, *Minutes*, November 20, 1904, December 4, 1904, and January 8, 1905.

23. *Record-Herald*, April 1 and April 29, 1905; Philip, "Chicago and the Downstate," pp. 173–74.

24. Chicago, *Journal of the Proceedings of the City Council*, May 15, 1905, pp. 209–10.

25. Ibid., June 12, 1905, pp. 551–52, and June 19, 1905, p. 633; *Record-Herald*, June 20, 1905.

26. *Record-Herald*, June 20, 1905.

27. The information on the delegates was compiled from Chicago Charter Convention, *Officers, List of Delegates, Rules and Committees*, pamphlet, Chicago Historical Society; Daily *News, Almanac*, (1906); the Illinois *Blue Book* (1905); and Marquis, *Book of Chicagoans* (1905 and 1911).

28. See for example, Chicago Charter Convention, *Proceedings*, March 1, 1907, pp. 1200–1201, and Michael McCarthy, "Businessmen and Professionals in Municipal Reform: The Chicago Experience, 1887–1920" (Ph.D. Diss., Northwestern University, 1970).

29. Walter L. Fisher to Governor Charles Deneen, September 11,

1905, Walter L. Fisher Papers, box no. 6, Library of Congress, Washington, D.C.

3. The Charter Convention

1. See Charles Beard, *American City Government: A Survey of Newer Tendencies* (New York: Century, 1912); Richard M. Bernard and Bradley R. Rice, "Political Environment and the Adoption of Progressive Municipal Reform," *Journal of Urban History* 1 (1975): 149–74; Ernest Griffith, *A History of American City Government: The Progressive Years and Their Aftermath, 1900–1920* (New York: Praeger, 1974); Martin Schiesl, *The Politics of Efficiency: Municipal Administration and Reform in America, 1880–1920* (Berkeley: University of California, 1977).

2. Chicago Charter Convention, *Proceedings*, December 3, 1906, p. 90; December 10, pp. 209–14, 217; and December 11, pp. 238–40; and Walter L. Fisher to M. L. McKinley (convention secretary), May 16, 1906, Walter L. Fisher Papers, box no. 6, Library of Congress, Washington, D.C.

3. Hoyt King, "The Reform Movement in Chicago," *The Annals* 25 (March 1905): 235–47.

4. Charles E. Merriam, *Chicago: A More Intimate View of Urban Politics* (New York: Macmillan, 1929), pp. 21–22, 263–67.

5. Walter L. Fisher to Leverett L. Lyon, March 12, 1906, Walter Fisher Papers, box no. 6; Lincoln Steffens, *The Shame of the Cities* (New York: S. S. McClure, 1902), pp. 164–65.

6. See, for example, Charles Merriam to G. A. Cuthbertson, October 17, 1907, and Charles Merriam to Lloyd L. Maurer, April 10, 1908, in Charles E. Merriam Papers, folders no. 9 and 26, University of Chicago.

7. Chicago *Tribune*, April 4, 1900.

8. For instance, in the mayoral campaign that followed the closing of the charter convention in the spring of 1907, the Republican party blithely equated its candidate and platform with nonpartisan politics, despite ample evidence to the contrary. See Maureen A. Flanagan, "Fred A. Busse: A Silent Mayor for Turbulent Times," in *Chicago Political Tradition*, ed. Paul M. Green and Melvin Holli (Carbondale: Southern Illinois University Press, 1987), for an example of this in the 1907 mayoral campaign.

9. For instance, in 1898, the MVL claimed that 19 of its 22 aldermanic candidates were elected; in 1899, 25 were elected; in 1900, with another 19 elected, the group figured that 42 of the 70 aldermen were

sympathetic to the league's concern for honest government. See *Trib-une*, April 5, 1898, April 4, 1899, and April 4, 1900. See also, Michael McCarthy, "The New Metropolis: Chicago, The Annexation Movement, and Progressive Reform," in *The Age of Urban Reform: New Perspectives on the Progressive Era*, ed. Michael Ebner and Eugene Tobin (Port Washington: Kennikat, 1977), pp. 43–54.

10. In this sense, I cannot agree with Michael McCarthy's assessment that the MVL victories occurred because "Chicagoans found themselves dealing with issues that cut across the traditional social barriers and created new, broad-based coalitions. . . . they made the 'new citizenry' work." See McCarthy, "The New Metropolis," pp. 50–51.

11. See King, "Reform Movement in Chicago," pp. 235, 239.

12. Replying to a letter from M. H. Lebensohn, in which Lebensohn expressed his concern that the charter as written would make it easy for some political machine to redistrict the wards and take control of the city, Walter Fisher expressed supreme confidence that the people of Chicago would never allow this to happen. "No matter how they divide the wards, in my opinion, the people would drive them out of power." Fisher to M. H. Lebensohn, September 14, 1907, Fisher Papers, box no. 6. But when the charter was defeated a few days later, Fisher could not contain his bitterness, saying that the charter "was beaten because of a 'combination of selfishness and stupidity with which every constructive movement has to contend.'" Chicago *Record-Herald*, September 18, 1907.

13. Charter Convention, *Proceedings*, December 11, 1906, pp. 242–46, 249.

14. Ibid., February 18, 1907, p. 941.

15. Civic Federation of Chicago, "Preliminary Report on the Need for a New City Charter," in Civic Federation Papers, box no. 3, Chicago Historical Society.

16. Chicago Federation of Labor, *Minutes*, January 8, 1905. See also Chicago, *Journal of the Proceedings of the City Council*, January 2, 1906, pp. 2014–20 for a charter plan submitted to that body by one of the aldermen, under which Chicago would have been given strong home-rule powers; and the Chicago *Daily Socialist*, January 10, 1906, for a similar plan.

17. Charter Convention, *Proceedings*, December 13, 1906, p. 296.

18. Ibid., pp. 297–99.

19. Ibid., December 6, 1906, p. 190.

20. Ibid., December 3, 1906, p. 114, and December 10, 1906, p. 208.

21. See Flanagan, "Fred A. Busse."

22. *Tribune*, March 23, 1907, and April 3, 1907.

23. *Daily News, Almanac,* 1903, p.364, and 1905, p. 356.

24. CFL, *Minutes,* December 2, 1906, and December 16, 1906; Charter Convention, *Proceedings,* December 17, 1906, p. 406.

25. Charter Convention, *Proceedings,* December 17, 1906, pp. 378–79, 385–88.

26. Ibid., December 17, 1906, pp. 410–412, and March 1, 1907, p. 1160.

27. The exact wording of the amendment read: "The General Assembly shall have power . . . to pass any law . . . providing a scheme or charter of local municipal government for the territory now or hereafter embraced with the limits of the City of Chicago. The law or laws so passed . . . may provide for the assessment of property and the levy and collection of taxes within said city for corporate purposes in accordance with the principles of equality and uniformity prescribed by this Constitution." Illinois Constitution (1870) article 4, section 34.

28. Charter Convention, *Proceedings,* October 3, 1906, pp. 7–8, and December 18, 1906, p. 467.

29. Ibid., December 18, 1906, p. 468.

30. Charles Merriam, *Report of an Investigation of the Municipal Revenues of Chicago* (Chicago: City Club of Chicago, 1906), esp. pp. 94–95; Charter Convention, *Proceedings,* October 3, 1906, p. 8, and December 19, pp. 526–28.

31. Ibid., December 19, 1906, pp. 528–30, and December 20, pp. 558–61. The ten appointees of the legislature who were at this session all voted against Merriam's proposal, but even without their negative votes, this resolution would not have passed. The CFL had made adoption of a municipal tax system one of the points of its home-rule resolution. See CFL, *Minutes,* January 8, 1905. And in a public-policy vote in November 1904, Chicago voters had approved by a three to one margin a proposal seeking to give local governments authority to adopt whatever system of assessing and levying taxes that they wanted. *Daily News, Almanac,* 1905, p. 356.

32. Charter Convention, *Proceedings,* December 18, 1906, p. 464, and February 25, 1907, pp. 1044–52.

33. Ibid., October 3, 1906, p. 2.

34. *Tribune,* April 6, 1896.

35. CFL, *Minutes,* December 2, 1906, and *Record-Herald,* December 3, 1906.

36. Margaret Dreier Robins to Lincoln Steffens, November 6, 1906, printed in Mary E. Dreier, *Margaret Dreier Robins: Her Life, Letters, and Work* (New York: 1950), p. 96.

37. "Report of the Committee on Public Education," April 1, 1907, pp. 34–35, in City Club of Chicago Papers, Chicago Historical Society.

38. Merriam, *Chicago*, p. 128.

39. Charter Convention, *Proceedings*, December 20, 1906, p. 561. In 1904, the voters had approved by a margin of two to one, a nonbinding public-policy measure to make membership on the board of education elective rather than appointive. *Daily News, Almanac*, 1905, p. 385.

40. Charter Convention, *Proceedings*, December 20, 1906, pp. 569, 572–74, 582–83.

41. Ibid., December 21, 1906, pp. 620, 622–23.

42. Ibid., pp. 624–25.

43. Ibid., December 26, 1906, pp. 717–18.

44. Ibid., pp. 722–24, 727. Post also published his ideas in *The Public*, November 17, 1906, and later wrote more extensively about them in his unpublished autobiography, "Living a Long Life Over," in Louis Post Papers, Library of Congress, Washington, D.C.

45. Charter Convention, *Proceedings*, December 21, 1906, p. 614.

46. Wayne Urban, "Progressive Education in the Urban South: Reform of the Atlanta Schools, 1914–1918," in *The Age of Urban Reform*, ed. Ebner and Tobin, pp. 134–35.

47. *The Public*, November 17, 1906; Adade Wheeler and Marlene Wortman, *The Roads They Made: Women in Illinois History* (Chicago: Charles Kerr, 1977), pp. 87–89.

48. See above, chapter 1.

49. Regarding Haley, see for example, *Tribune*, March 22, 1907, and March 30. Charter Convention, *Proceedings*, December 20, 1906, pp. 572–74; Wheeler and Wortman, *The Roads They Made*, pp. 86–89 and 106.

50. CFL, *Minutes*, April 1, 1906; Chicago Woman's Club, *Minutes of Board Meetings*, September 26, 1906, in Chicago Woman's Club Papers, Chicago Historical Society.

51. Jane Addams, *Twenty Years at Hull-House* (New York: Macmillan, 1910), p. 237.

52. Ibid., pp. 203–6, 237–38.

53. Illinois Association Opposed to the Extension of Suffrage to Women, *A Protest against the Granting of Municipal Suffrage to Women in the City of Chicago*, pamphlet, Chicago Historical Society.

54. Catherine Waugh McCullough to Raymond Robins, November 30, 1906, in Raymond Robins Papers, State Historical Society of Wisconsin, Madison, Wisconsin; Charter Convention, *Proceedings*, December 4, 1906, pp. 130–31.

55. Charter Convention, *Proceedings*, December 4, 1906, pp. 130–32; *The Public*, January 5, 1907.

56. Charter Convention, *Proceedings*, December 27, 1906, pp. 767–72, 776.

57. Ibid., December 27, 1906, p. 778.

58. Ibid., pp. 771–72, 778, 783.

59. Catherine Waugh McCullough to Raymond Robins, January 8 and January 14, 1907, in Robins Papers; Charter Convention, *Proceedings*, February 16, 1907, pp. 890–91.

60. *Abendpost*, May 28, 1906.

61. John Buenker, "The Dynamics of Chicago Ethnic Politics, 1900–1931," *Journal of the Illinois State Historical Society* 67 (April 1974): 175–99; Buenker, "The Illinois Legislature and Prohibition, 1907–1919," *The Journal of the Illinois State Historical Society* 62 (Winter 1969): 363–84; Paul Kleppner, *The Cross of Culture: A Social Analysis of Midwestern Politics, 1850–1900* (New York: The Free Press, 1970).

62. *Abendpost*, December 3 and December 4, 1906; Charter Convention, *Proceedings*, December 6, 1906, p. 190. For accounts of the continuing strength of antiprohibition sentiment in Chicago in the succeeding years see Alex Gottfried, *Boss Cermak of Chicago: A Study of Political Leadership* (Seattle: University of Washington, 1962), pp. 83–84, 101–2.

63. Charter Convention, *Proceedings*, December 13, 1906, pp. 346–47, and December 18, 1906, p. 491.

64. Illinois, Cities and Villages Act, 1872, article 1, section 6 and article 5, section 1; Illinois, Laws, ch. 38, rev. stat. 1845, sec. 259; Charter Convention, *Proceedings*, December 26, 1906, pp. 712–14.

65. CFL, *Minutes*, December 16, 1906; *Abendpost*, December 17, 1906.

66. *Abendpost*, December 24, 1906.

67. Robert McCurdy to Raymond Robins, December 3, 1906, in Robins Papers. Such a law did pass in 1907, and the Chicago temperance forces took credit for helping to design and pass the new law. See J. C. Jackson, "The Work of the Anti-Saloon League," *The Annals* 32 (1908): 486–92.

68. McCurdy to Robins, December 3, 1906.

69. *Abendpost*, December 22, 1906.

70. *Abendpost*, December 24, 1906; United Societies for Local Self-Government, *Home Rule Bulletin* 3 (January 5, 1907).

71. Charter Convention, *Proceedings*, December 27, 1906, pp. 786–90, 792–93.

72. The logic of Rosenthal's argument is obscure; nevertheless, this was his stated position. Ibid., pp. 791–92, 794.

73. See above, chapter 1, for discussion of the franchise problem in Chicago up to the time of the convention.

74. See especially Walter L. Fisher to John V. Farwell, February 13, 1906, in Fisher Papers, box no. 6.

75. Charter Convention, *Proceedings*, December 14, 1906, pp. 338–39.

76. Ibid., pp. 339–42.

77. See Ibid., December 14, 1906, pp. 339–42, and February 23, 1907, pp. 1015–18. Six of the twenty delegates voting on both, voted to repeal rights of frontage consents and to give the council this power to enforce the tenement ordinances.

78. Ibid., March 1, 1907, pp. 1173–79. Earlier in the convention, when they had passed the bulk of the provisions on public utilities, several of the delegates had insisted upon retaining a careful distinction between right to own and right to operate. See Ibid., December 14, 1906, pp. 336–37.

79. Ibid., December 17, 1906, pp. 415, 417–18.

80. Ibid., March 1, 1907, pp. 1143, 1148–49.

81. Ibid., March 1, 1907, pp. 1200–1201.

82. Ibid., pp. 1193–94.

83. Ibid., p. 1194.

84. Ibid., pp. 1192, 1199.

4. The Charter and the Politicians

1. There were three prevailing factions in both the Democratic and Republican parties at this time. See Charles Merriam, *Chicago: A More Intimate View of Urban Politics* (New York: Macmillan, 1929), pp. 94–97.

2. George C. Sikes, "Chicago's New Mayor," *The American Monthly Review of Reviews* (May 1907): 585.

3. See Maureen A. Flanagan, "Fred A. Busse: A Silent Mayor for Turbulent Times," in *The Chicago Political Tradition*, ed. Melvin Holli and Paul Green (Carbondale: Southern Illinois University Press, 1987) for an account of the election campaign.

4. The Chicago *Tribune*, March 22, 1907.

5. Ibid., March 23 and March 29, 1907.

6. Ibid., March 26, 1907.

7. See Chicago Federation of Labor, *Minutes*, January and February, 1907.

8. *Tribune*, March 29, 1907.

9. Sikes, "Chicago's New Mayor," p. 588, and *Tribune*, March 20, 1907.

10. For examples, see *Tribune*, March 23, March 26, March 28, and April 1, 1907.

11. Ibid., March 29, 1907.

12. Ibid., March 23, March 28, and March 27, 1907.

13. Ibid., March 23, March 26, and March 24, 1907.

14. Ibid., editorial, March 22, 1907. The newspaper's hatred of Margaret Haley, head of the Chicago Teachers' Federation, and her supposed connections with city hall was displayed constantly during the campaign. See for examples, March 22, 1907, where she is derisively referred to as "Deputy Assistant Mayor," and March 30, 1907, where she is accussed of bringing politicking to the schools. The newspaper seems to have conveniently forgotten that the Civic Federation tried to use the schools for its charter amendment campaign three years earlier.

15. Ibid., March 31, 1907.

16. Ibid., March 21 and March 23, 1907.

17. *Abendpost*, April 1 and 3, 1907.

18. Editorial in *Tribune*, April 3, 1907.

19. Illinois, House *Journal*, May 2, 1907, pp. 896–97.

20. William B. Philip, "Chicago and the Downstate: A Study of Their Conflicts, 1870–1934" (Ph.D. Diss., University of Chicago, 1940), p. 158.

21. Ibid., pp. 62–63. Similar attempts to limit representation had failed in 1901, when all the negative votes except one in the Senate were cast by Cook County representatives; and in 1903, when the House tabled the measure 75–62, with 57 negatives registered from Cook County. Ibid., pp. 54–58.

22. Ibid., pp. 176–77, 270–72; J. C. Jackson, "The Work of the Anti-Saloon League," *The Annals* 32 (1908): 485.

23. The original version of the charter, as passed by the convention, and the final version, as amended by the legislature, can be found in the Charter Convention, *Proceedings*, at the Municipal Reference Library, Chicago, Illinois. The amended version is also printed in Illinois, Senate *Journal* (1907): 1079–1160.

24. Chicago Charter Convention, *Proceedings*, December 3, 1906, pp. 98–99, 102–4, 111; CFL, *Minutes*, April 15, 1906; and *Daily News, Almanac*, 1905, p. 356, for results of the public-policy vote favoring the direct primary. The Illinois legislature did institute a state direct primary law in 1910.

25. *Tribune*, May 18, 1907.

26. Harding was not among the original twelve, but as a board member described as voting "repeatedly for [Chicago] federation [of Teachers] measures," he soon followed. Ibid., May 18 and May 25, 1907; and CFL, *Minutes*, June 16, 1907.

27. *Tribune*, May 18, 1907.

28. Ibid., May 28, 1907.

29. *The Public*, May 18, 1907.

5. The Campaign to Ratify the Charter

1. Chicago Federation of Labor, *Minutes*, June 16, 1907; Civic Federation of Chicago, *The New Chicago Charter: Why It Should Be Adopted at the Special Election, September 17th*, pamphlet, Chicago Historical Society; for the Federation of Teachers, see Chicago *American*, June 16, 1907; for Post and the Independence League, see *The Public*, May 18, 1907, and the *American*, June 7 and June 12, 1907; for Merriam, see Chicago *Record-Herald*, July 3, July 9, and July 12, 1907, and a series of ten articles on "What Chicago's Proposed Charter Means," beginning in the Chicago *Daily News*, August 26, 1907; for Fisher, see Walter L. Fisher to Governor Deneen, May 16, 1907, Walter L. Fisher Papers, box no. 6, Library of Congress; for Foreman's fundraising activities, see the *American*, July 7, 1907; and for the United Societies, see *Abendpost*, May 27, 1907.

2. City Club of Chicago, "Home Rule Features of the New City Charter," City Club *Bulletin* 1 (June 19, 1907): 147.

3. Ibid., pp. 148–52.

4. See especially his article in Chicago *Record-Herald*, July 3, 1907.

5. Civic Federation of Chicago, *The New Chicago Charter: Why It Should Be Adopted at the Special Election, September 17th*, pp. 1, 9. In this pamphlet the Civic Federation was primarily addressing, without mentioning them by name, the CFL and United Societies. See *Abendpost*, May 27, 1907, for complete text of coverage of the United Societies' convention, with an explanation of the organization's complete position on home rule and its opposition to the parks' consolidation as conceived in this charter.

6. Charles Merriam, "Home Rule in Chicago's New Charter," *The Voter* (July 1907): 24–31.

7. City Club, "Home Rule Features," p. 153.

8. *Abendpost*, May 27, 1907.

9. City Club, "Home Rule Features," pp. 153–56.

10. Civic Federation, *The New Chicago Charter*, p. 9. See also

Milton J. Foreman, "Chicago New Charter Movement—Its Relation to Municipal Ownership," *The Annals* 31 (May 1908): 105–14, for the same lack of understanding of the differing positions.

11. United Societies for Local Self-Government, *Seven Reasons to Vote against the Charter*, pamphlet, reprinted in Illinois *Staats-Zeitung*, August 1, 1907. The original German reads "Die Macht, den Charter durch öffentliche Abstimmung abzuändern, wird ausdrücklich verweigert hinsichtlich der Besteuerung, der öffentlichen Nutzbarkeiten, des Erziehungswesens und aller Angelegenheiten, welche die Wohlfahrt unserer Gesellschaften und die persönlichen Rechte und Freiheiten des Volkes von Chicago empfindlich berühren." I have located no extant copies of this pamphlet and did not find it reprinted in any of the major daily newspapers, but only in the Black newspaper the *Broad-Ax*, August 24, 1907. It was, however, quoted from by other people in the city and referred to in the *Record-Herald*, August 9, 1907.

12. United Societies, *Seven Reasons*.

13. See for example, Robert A. Caro, *The Power Broker: Robert Moses and the Fall of New York* (New York: Knopf, 1974); and Jon C. Teaford, *The Twentieth-Century American City: Problem, Promise and Reality* (Baltimore: Johns Hopkins, 1986), pp. 48–56.

14. City Club of Chicago, "Revenue Provisions of the Proposed City Charter," City Club *Bulletin* 1 (June 26, 1907): 157, 161, 162.

15. Clifton K. Yearley, *The Money Machines: The Breakdown and Reform of Governmental and Party Finance in the North, 1860–1920* (Albany: State University of New York, 1970).

16. In recognition of this facet of fiscal reform, Walter Fisher wrote to Governor Deneen urging the governor not to veto the repeal of the Juul Law. The Juul Law had set the existing tax limits, and if it was repealed, there would be no limit. Fisher thought that the absence of a limit would make the charter, with its definite limits on taxation, more attractive to Chicago property owners. Walter L. Fisher to Governor Deneen, May 16, 1907, in Fisher Papers, box no. 6.

17. Civic Federation, *The New Chicago Charter*, pp. 1–2.

18. Ibid., pp. 2, 11.

19. CFL, *Minutes*, July 21, 1907. The committee report was also printed in labor's monthly journal, the *Union Labor Advocate* (August 1907).

20. See Chicago Charter Convention, *Proceedings*, December 18, 1906, pp. 471–81.

21. CFL, *Minutes*, July 21, 1907, and *Record-Herald*, July 22, 1907. See also CFL, *Minutes*, June 16, 1907, for some of the first ver-

sions of the organization's arguments before they were developed as a whole into this committee report.

22. CFL, *Minutes*, July 21, 1907, and August 4, 1907. The CFL report warned that the city's enhanced police powers to arrest and detain people for disturbing the peace could easily be used against political or labor rallies or against strikers, especially if businessmen controlled the municipal government, and that the provision authorizing the city to examine and license workers also could be used against workers to thwart union organizing and strikes. See also Chicago *American*, July 8, 1907, for an earlier voicing of this concern.

23. See, for example, Charles Beard, *The Rise of American Civilization* (New York: 1927), and Vernon L. Parrington, *Main Currents of American Thought* (New York: 1927–1930).

24. See, for example, Richard Hofstadter, *The Age of Reform* (New York: 1955), and Otis Pease, "Urban Reformers in the Progressive Era: A Reassessment," *Pacific Northwest Quarterly* 62 (1971): 49–58.

25. Among other things, the Independence League aimed to prevent private confiscation of public property, to secure majority rule of the municipal government, and to prosecute the frauds perpetrated by great financial organizations. See *The Public*, July 14, 1906.

26. David Nord, "The Public Community: The Urbanization of Journalism in Chicago," *Journal of Urban History* (August 1985): 430.

27. The *American* was the counterpart, in a sense, to the *Tribune*. While the latter could always be counted on to tout the line of business, the managing editor of the former, A. M. Lawrence, was a leading figure in the Independence League. When used side by side on an issue such as the charter, the two newspapers are quite useful for providing a comparative context and opposing argumentation.

28. *American*, editorial, June 12, 1907.

29. Ibid., July 5, 1907.

30. Ibid., July 4, 1907.

31. Ibid., editorial, July 11, 1907.

32. See Michael McCarthy, "Businessmen and Professionals in Municipal Reform: The Chicago Experience, 1887–1920" (Ph.D. Diss., Northwestern University, 1970) and Martin Schiesl, *The Politics of Efficiency: Municipal Administration and Reform in America, 1880–1920* (Berkeley: University of California, 1977). Both works build on the general interpretation of the Progressive Era advanced by Robert Wiebe in *Businessmen and Reform* (Cambridge: Harvard University, 1962) and *The Search for Order, 1877–1920* (New York: Hill and Wang, 1967).

33. *American*, August 7, 1907.

34. *Staats-Zeitung*, August 1, 1907.

35. *American-Sunday Examiner*, July 7, 1907.

36. See *Tribune* articles each day from March 26 to postelection day April 3, 1907, for examples.

37. Ibid., March 29, 1907.

38. Ibid.

39. *American*, August 4, 1907.

40. Louise DeKoven Bowen, *Growing Up with a City* (New York: Macmillan, 1926), pp. 106–7.

41. *Inter-Ocean*, September 9, 1907.

42. Jane Addams, *Twenty Years at Hull-House* (New York: Macmillan, 1910), p. 237.

43. This sense of powerlessnes to control their own affairs in the city was felt acutely by the largely female constituency of the Chicago Federation of Teachers, who believed that they and the schools would suffer badly under the proposed charter. The union authorized a committee to work with other women's groups opposing the charter. See Chicago *American*, June 16, 1907.

44. This approach was first fully articulated by Melvin Holli, *Reform in Detroit: Hazen S. Pingree and Urban Politics* (New York: Oxford, 1969), in his analysis of social reformers in Detroit in the Progressive Era. For the same type of methodology applied to structural reformers see Martin Schiesl, *The Politics of Efficiency*. But by studying the actions and ideas of one segment of urban residents in isolation from others, calling them either social of structural reformers, both authors emphasize the definition of the two terms in opposition to one another and we receive an incomplete picture of the urban context and interactions among people of differing ideas.

45. See above, chapter 3, for his position on various charter provisions at the convention, and chapter 4, for his role in the school board crisis.

46. The heading of one of two untitled pages in Raymond Robins Papers, box 42, vol. 3, at the State Historical Society of Wisconsin, wherein he outlined his reasons for opposing the charter.

47. Text of the speech printed in Public Policy League, *Bulletin* 1 (September 1907), copy in Charles Merriam Papers, box 72, folder 10 at University of Chicago.

48. *American*, July 19, 1907.

49. City Club of Chicago, "Political Features of the Proposed City Charter," City Club *Bulletin* 1 (July 10, 1907): 167 and 173.

50. Ibid., pp. 165–66.

51. Ibid., pp. 165, 167.

52. John Buenker, "The Dynamics of Chicago Ethnic Politics, 1900–1930," *Journal of the Illinois State Historical Society* 67 (April 1974): 182.

53. Ibid., p. 170.

54. CFL, *Minutes*, July 21, 1907; *Union Labor Advocate* (August 1907).

55. United Societies, *Seven Reasons to Vote against the Charter*; *Abendpost*, May 27, 1907; and *Staats-Zeitung*, September 7, 1907.

56. Public Policy League, *Bulletin* 1 and Raymond Robins Papers, box 42, vol. 3; *The Public*, May 18, 1907; and *American*, June 12, 1907.

57. Quoted in Buenker, "The Dynamics of Chicago Ethnic Politics," p. 188. See also Joel Tarr, *A Study in Boss Politics: William Lorimer of Chicago* (Urbana: University of Illinois, 1971).

58. CFL, *Minutes*, April 15, 1906. The organization later listed the charter provision that "re-establishes the old primary law which leaves candidate selection to the bosses," as one of its reasons for opposing the charter. Ibid., July 21, 1907. See City Club of Chicago, *Bulletin* 1 (June 19, 1907): 153–56, for Edward Noonan's statement on the United Societies' position in this question.

59. CFL, *Minutes*, March 3, 1907, and July 21, 1907; United Societies for Local Self-Government, *Seven Reasons to Vote against the Charter*; *Staats-Zeitung*, September 5 and September 15, 1907; *Record-Herald*, September 17, 1907; and *Inter-Ocean*, September 6, 1907. See also the arguments on the civil service issue at the convention, Chicago Charter Convention, *Proceedings*, December 6, 1906, pp. 157–58, and particularly James Linehan's observations regarding the exemption of the municipal court employees, p. 162.

60. Civic Federation, *The New Chicago Charter*, p. 9.

61. See the *Inter-Ocean*, September 6, 1907, for a lengthy anticharter speech made by Dunne, and September 15, 1907, for the speeches of William O'Connell and William Dever, both important members of that faction of the party.

62. Under the auspices of O'Connell and Dunne, the Committee issued its own anti-charter pamphlet. See Cook County Democratic Central Committee, *Reasons Why the Proposed Charter Should Be Defeated*. The only copy of this pamphlet that I was able to locate was in the Charles Merriam Papers, box 72, folder 10. Also, *American*, July 10, 1907, for the list of the Democratic Central Committee anticharter committee.

63. Paul M. Green, "Irish Chicago: The Multiethnic Road to Ma-

chine Success," in *Ethnic Chicago*, ed. Peter d'A. Jones and Melvin Holli (Grand Rapids: Eerdmans, 1981), pp. 227–28; and John Buenker, "Edward F. Dunne: The Urban New Stock Democrat as Progressive," *Mid-America* 50 (January 1968): 3–21.

64. *Inter-Ocean*, September 17, 1907; *American-Sunday Examiner*, August 11, 1907; and *American*, July 25, 1907.

65. City Club, *Bulletin* 1 (July 10, 1907): 172.

66. See above, chapter 3.

67. Republican party bosses Fred Busse and William Lorimer supported the charter.

68. *Staats-Zeitung*, August 1, 1907. The newspaper reminded its readers that Berry also had had a hand in burying the separate liquor regulation bills that had gone to Springfield with the charter. Several days later, the newspaper also reported threats being made in the state to run Berry for governor on a Republican-Prohibition ticket if Chicagoans rejected the charter. Ibid., August 10, 1907.

69. Ibid., August 8, 1907.

70. *Tribune*, March 23, 1907.

71. *Abendpost*, September 5, 1907; *American*, September 6, 1907; and *Inter-Ocean*, September 6, 1907.

72. *Abendpost*, September 7, 1907; *Staats-Zeitung*, September 7 and September 8, 1907.

73. *Inter-Ocean*, September 14, 1907.

74. Ibid., September 14, 1907, and *Staats-Zeitung*, September 14, 1907.

75. *American-Sunday Examiner*, September 15, 1907.

76. See *Inter-Ocean*, September 10 and September 15, 1907.

77. *American-Sunday Examiner*, September 15, 1907.

78. *American-Sunday Examiner*, July 7, 1907.

79. *Staats-Zeitung*, September 8, August 27, and September 5, 1907.

80. *Staats-Zeitung*, September 16, 1907. See also September 14, 1907, regarding objections to taxation scheme, especially the bond issue, and September 15, 1907, on opposing the charter for its lack of home rule, ward redistricting, higher taxes, gutted school board and civil-service systems, and possibility of Sunday closings.

81. *Inter-Ocean*, September 14, 1907.

82. *Tribune*, editorial, September 16, 1907, and September 17, 1907; *Daily News*, editorial, September 16, 1907; *Record-Herald*, editorial, September 17, 1907.

83. *Daily News*, *Almanac* (1908), p. 495, gives the official ward-by-ward tally of the referendum vote.

6. Failure and Aftermath

1. Walter L. Fisher to M. H. Lebensohn, September 14, 1907, in Walter L. Fisher Papers, box no. 6, Library of Congress, Washington, D.C.

2. Chicago *Record-Herald*, September 18, 1907.

3. Chicago *Tribune*, September 18, 1907.

4. *Record-Herald*, September 18, 1907.

5. Charles Merriam to H. B. Chamberlain, October 11, 1907, in Charles Merriam Papers, box 12, folder 7, and Charles Merriam to G. A. Cuthbertson, October 17, 1907, box 12, folder 9, University of Chicago.

6. Milton Foreman, "The Chicago New Charter Movement—Its Relation to Municipal Ownership," *The Annals* 31 (May 1908): 1–2.

7. Chicago *American*, September 18, 1907.

8. *Record-Herald*, September 18, 1907.

9. *American*, September 18, 1907.

10. Chicago Federation of Labor, *Minutes*, October 6, 1907.

11. The actual development of farm-labor coalitions in other areas of the midwest, along with the explicit rhetoric of the people versus special interests being expressed at the time, lends credence to these kinds of statements by the CFL.

12. City Club of Chicago, "The Charter Situation—What Next?" City Club *Bulletin* 1 (October 23, 1907): 217–20.

13. Illinois *Staats-Zeitung*, September 18, 1907.

14. City Club, "The Charter Situation," pp. 215–17.

15. *Staats-Zeitung*, January 20, 1908.

16. *Record-Herald*, February 27, 1908, and March 22, 1908.

17. *Staats-Zeitung*, February 10, 1908.

18. *Record-Herald*, April 8, 1908.

19. The decision to involve the United Societies in the actual promotion of political candidates and to present members of the United Societies themselves for political offices remained a disputed one for a time within the organization. Not all members agreed upon this course, but over the next few years, the United Societies committed itself more and more strongly to political involvement. See the reports of the third and fourth annual conventions, in *Staats-Zeitung*, May 25, 1908, and *Abendpost*, May 24, 1909.

20. *Record-Herald*, September 4 and October 13, 1908.

21. CFL, *Minutes*, December 6 and December 20, 1908; published also in *Union Labor Advocate* (January 1909): 6, 11.

22. *Record-Herald*, October 28, 1908.

23. Ibid., November 13, 1908; Chicago Charter Convention, *An Act to Provide a Charter for the City of Chicago* (1909), articles 5-1, 12-1, 13-1, and 4, Chicago Historical Society.

24. Charles Merriam to Catherine W. McCullough, November 4, 1908, in Merriam Papers, box 12, folder 25.

25. *Record-Herald*, November 11, 1908. When the suffrage bill was ultimately sent to Springfield, the *Union Labor Advocate* urged that labor support the bill and told women workers to request that their unions pass a supporting resolution. *Union Labor Advocate* (April 1909): 31.

26. *Record-Herald*, December 1, 1908.

27. Chicago Charter Convention, *Resolutions and Communications Received at the Meeting Held January 29, 1909*, at Chicago Historical Society.

28. *Record-Herald*, December 1, 1908.

29. Charter Convention, *An Act to Provide a Charter* (1909), article 5–2 (amended) and articles 9–10 and 9–10a.

30. *Record-Herald*, February 8, 1909.

31. Ibid., February 23, 1909. Among them were bills on consolidation and revenue, home rule, Sunday closings, woman suffrage, and the public schools. See Ibid., May 3, 1909.

32. Ibid., March 16, 1909.

33. Ibid., March 24, 1909.

34. Ibid., April 29, 1909.

35. Ibid., May 1 and May 4, 1909.

36. William B. Philip, "Chicago and the Downstate: A Study of Their Conflicts, 1870–1934" (Ph.D. Diss., University of Chicago, 1940), pp. 66, 72, 178; *Record-Herald*, May 1 and May 14, 1909.

37. *Record-Herald*, May 14, 1909.

38. Ibid., May 20, 1909.

39. Chicago, *Journal of the Proceedings of the City Council*, July 22, 1912, p. 1644; January 20, 1913, p. 3353; February 14, 1913, p. 3730; and March 9, 1914, pp. 4362–63.

40. For details of the commission's work see *Proceedings of the Permanent Charter Commission* (1914–1915), at Municipal Reference Library, Chicago, Illinois and "Report of the Permanent Charter Commission to the City Council," contained in Chicago, *Journal of the City Council*, July 12, 1915, pp. 1126–28.

41. Hoyt King, *Citizen Cole of Chicago* (Chicago: 1931), pp. 133–42.

42. The CFL had continued to back such a process, recommending

to its members in 1918 to vote yes for a constitutional convention. See CFL, *Minutes,* November 3, 1918, and *Union Labor Advocate* (November 1918): 1.

43. CFL, *Minutes,* February 16, 1919.

44. See Janet Cornelius, *Constitution Making in Illinois, 1818–1970* (Urbana: University of Illinois Press, 1972), pp. 98–99.

45. Ibid., p. 108. For details of this issue at the convention, see *Journal of the Constitutional Convention* (1920–1922): 199–201, 210, 491–93.

46. See Philip, "Chicago and the Downstate," p. 108; for discussion of downstate opposition to any measure instituting statewide municipal home rule, ibid., p. 181.

47. Cornelius, *Constitution Making,* pp. 110–11.

Conclusion

1. Michael McCarthy, "Businessmen and Professionals in Municipal Reform: The Chicago Experience, 1887–1920" (Ph.D. Diss., Northwestern University, 1970), p. 190.

2. See Chicago *Tribune,* May 30, 1907, for this argument in detail.

3. The first quote is from Chicago Federation of Labor, *Minutes,* August 4, 1907; the second is from Ibid., May 16, 1909, reprinted in *Union Labor Advocate* (June 1909): 9.

4. The examples are numerous. Howard Gosnell, *Machine Politics: Chicago Model* (Chicago: University of Chicago Press, 1937), and Charles Merriam, *Chicago: A More Intimate View of Urban Politics* (New York: Macmillan, 1929), are two of the more prominent and influential works.

5. See, for example, Barry Karl, *Charles Merriam and the Study of Politics* (Chicago: University of Chicago, 1974).

6. The standard work on Cermak remains Alex Gottfried, *Boss Cermak of Chicago: A Study of Political Leadership* (Seattle: University of Washington, 1962). For this analysis of Cermak, the United Societies, and ethnic groups in general, see also, John Allswang, *A House for All Peoples: Ethnic Politics in Chicago, 1890–1936* (Lexington: University of Kentucky Press, 1971), and Paul Kleppner, *Chicago Divided: The Making of a Black Mayor* (DeKalb: Northern Illinois University Press, 1985), pp. 22–25. Discovering exactly what motivated Cermak, unfortunately, will prove extremely difficult, if not impossible. Gottfried told me that, in all his research on Cermak, he was never able to discover any of Cermak's personal papers and that the family simply did not wish to talk to anyone about him. Archie Motley, curator of the manu-

script collection at the Chicago Historical Society, confirmed that he has never been able to discover any personal papers.

7. John Buenker, "The Dynamics of Chicago Ethnic Politics, 1900–1930," *Journal of the Illinois State Historical Society* 67 (April 1974): 188.

8. *Union Labor Advocate*, editorial (April 1910): 34.

9. Ibid.

10. The *Union Labor Advocate* (March 31, 1911): 1, advocated Harrison as the friend of Labor, while Michael McCarthy, "Prelude to Armageddon: Charles E. Merriam and the Chicago Mayoral Election of 1911," *Journal of the Illinois State Historical Society* (November 1974): 513–14, cites much of organized labor backing Merriam for "his interest in reforms benefitting workingmen."

11. John Fitzpatrick was head of the CFL and ran for mayor on the Labor party ticket in 1919. See John Fitzpatrick Papers, box 8, file 56, Chicago Historical Society.

12. Typescript in Fitzpatrick papers, box 18, file 131, indicates segments of organized labor working for both candidates.

13. Paul Kleppner, *Chicago Divided: The Making of a Black Mayor*, pp. 20–22.

14. Alex Gottfried, *Boss Cermak*, pp. 212–16.

15. A recent example of the city's powerlessness to control these governing bodies occurred in October 1986. The city council was forced to ratify a new tax levy for the junior-college district. Many aldermen did not want to ratify this tax increase because it came right after a property-tax increase, but they admitted they had no legal choice in the matter.

16. Chicago Charter Convention, *Proceedings*, February 25, 1907, pp. 1065–66.

17. *Tribune*, April 16, 1980.

BIBLIOGRAPHY

Manuscript Collections

Chicago Federation of Teachers Papers. Chicago Historical Society.
Chicago Woman's Club Papers. Chicago Historical Society.
City Club of Chicago Papers. Chicago Historical Society.
Civic Federation of Chicago Papers. Chicago Historical Society.
Walter L. Fisher Papers. Manuscript Division, Library of Congress.
John Fitzpatrick Papers. Chicago Historical Society.
Charles E. Merriam Papers. University of Chicago.
Louis F. Post Papers. Manuscript Division, Library of Congress.
Raymond Robins Papers. State Historical Society of Wisconsin.

Newspapers, Almanacs, and Directories

Abendpost
The *Broad-Ax*
Chicago *American* and *Sunday Examiner*
Chicago *Daily News*
Chicago *Daily News, Almanac,* 1902–1909.
Chicago *Daily Socialist*
Chicago *Inter-Ocean*
Chicago *Record-Herald*
Chicago *Tribune*
Illinois *Blue Book,* 1905–1907.
Illinois *Staats-Zeitung*
L'Italia

Albert N. Marquis, ed. *Book of Chicagoans: A Biographical Dictionary of Leading Living Men of the City of Chicago,* 1905 and 1911.

The Public: A Journal of Democracy

Union Labor Advocate

Official Publications and Records

Chicago Charter Convention, 1906–1907. *An Act to Provide a Charter for the City of Chicago,* 1907.

––––––. *A Bill for an Act to Provide a Charter for the City of Chicago,* 1907.

––––––. *Officers, List of Delegates, Rules and Committees,* 1905.

––––––. *Proceedings,* October 1906–March 1907.

Chicago Charter Convention, 1908–1909. *An Act to Provide a Charter for the City of Chicago,* 1909.

––––––. *Resolutions and Communications Received at the Meeting Held January 29, 1909.*

Chicago Department of Health. *Bienniel Report,* 1895–1896.

Chicago Federation of Labor. *Minutes,* 1902–1919.

Chicago New Charter Convention, 1902–1903. *List of Delegates.*

––––––. *Proceedings,* 1902–1903.

Chicago Permanent Charter Commission, 1914–1915. *Proceedings,* 1914–1915.

Chicago Woman's Club. *Board Minutes,* 1906–1907.

City Club of Chicago. *Civic Committee Reports,* 1906–1907.

City of Chicago. *Journal of the Proceedings of the Chicago City Council,* 1900–1907 and 1912–1915.

Illinois. Cities and Villages Act, 1872.

––––––. Constitution, 1870.

––––––. House *Journal,* 1903 and 1907.

––––––. *Journal of the Constitutional Convention,* 1920–1922.

––––––. Senate *Journal,* 1903 and 1907.

United Societies for Local Self-Government. *Constitution and By-Laws.*

Articles, Books, and Pamphlets

Addams, Jane. "Problems of Municipal Administration." *American Journal of Sociology* 10 (1905): 425–44.

––––––. *Twenty Years at Hull-House.* New York, 1910.

Allswang, John M. *A House for All Peoples: Ethnic Politics in Chicago, 1890–1936.* Kentucky, 1971.

Angle, Paul M., ed. *Prairie State: Impressions of Illinois, 1673–1967, by Travelers and Other Observers.* Chicago, 1968.

Avrich, Paul. *The Haymarket Tragedy.* Princeton, 1984.

Barrett, Paul. *The Automobile and Urban Transit: The Formation of Public Policy in Chicago, 1900–1930.* Philadelphia, 1983.

Beard, Charles. *American City Government: A Survey of Newer Tendencies.* New York, 1912.

———. *The Rise of American Civilization.* New York, 1927.

Bernard, Richard, and Bradley Rice. "Political Environment and the Adoption of Progressive Municipal Reform." *Journal of Urban History* 2 (1975): 149–71.

Bowen, Louise DeKoven. *Growing Up with a City.* New York, 1926.

Buder, Stanley. *Pullman: An Experiment in Industrial Order and Community Planning, 1880–1930.* New York, 1967.

Buenker, John D. "The Dynamics of Chicago Ethnic Politics, 1900–1930." *Journal of the Illinois State Historical Society* 67 (1974): 175–99.

———. "Edward F. Dunne: The Urban New Stock Democrat as Progressive." *Mid-America* 50 (1968): 3–21.

———. "The Illinois Legislature and Prohibition, 1907–1919." *Journal of the Illinois State Historical Society* 62 (1969): 363–84.

———. *Urban Liberalism and Progressive Reform.* New York, 1973.

Caro, Robert A. *The Power Broker: Robert Moses and the Fall of New York.* New York, 1974.

Cerillo, Augustus. "The Reform of Municipal Government in New York City: From Seth Low to John Puroy Mitchel." *New York Historical Society Quarterly* 57 (June 1973): 51–71.

"The Charter Situation—What Next?" The City Club *Bulletin* 1 (October 1907): 212–20.

Chicago New Charter Movement. *Why the Pending Constitutional Amendment Should Be Adopted.* 1904 [at Chicago Historical Society].

Chudacoff, Howard. *The Evolution of American Urban Society.* Englewood Cliffs, 1975.

City of Chicago. *Historic City: The Settlement of Chicago.* Chicago, 1976.

Civic Federation of Chicago. *The New Chicago Charter. Why It Should Be Adopted at the Special Election, September 17th.* 1907 [at Chicago Historical Society].

———. *Preliminary Report on Need for New City Charter.* 1902 [at Chicago Historical Society].

Clayton, John. "The Scourge of Sinners: Arthur Burrage Farwell." *Chicago History* (1974): 68–77.

Conzen, Kathleen Neils. "Quantification and the New Urban History." *Journal of Interdisciplinary History* (1983): 653–78.

Cook County Democratic Central Committee. *Reasons Why the Proposed Charter Should Be Defeated.* 1907 [in Charles Merriam Papers, box 72].

Cornelius, Janet. *Constitution Making in Illinois, 1818–1970.* Urbana, 1972.

David, Henry. *The History of the Haymarket Affair.* New York, 1936.

Dillon, John F. *Commentaries on the Law of Municipal Corporations.* Boston, 1911.

Dreier, Mary. *Margaret Dreier Robins: Her Life, Letters and Work.* New York, 1950.

Eaton, Amasa. "The Right to Local Self-Government." *Harvard Law Review* 13–14 (1900–1901).

Ebner, Michael, and Eugene Tobin, eds. *The Age of Urban Reform: New Perspectives on the Progressive Era.* Port Washington, 1977.

Embree, Frances B. "The Housing of the Poor in Chicago." *Journal of Political Economy* 8 (1900): 354–77.

Evenson, Norma. *Paris, A Century of Change: 1878–1978.* New Haven, 1979.

Flanagan, Maureen A. "Charter Reform in Chicago: Political Culture and Urban Progressive Reform." *Journal of Urban History* 12 (1986): 109–30.

———. "The Ethnic Entry into Chicago Politics: The United Societies for Local Self-Government and the Reform Charter of 1907." *Journal of the Illinois State Historical Society* 75 (1982): 2–14.

———. "Fred A. Busse: A Silent Mayor in Turbulent Times." In *The Chicago Political Tradition,* edited by Paul M. Green and Melvin Holli. Carbondale, 1987.

Foreman, Milton J. "Chicago New Charter Movement—Its Relation to Municipal Ownership." *The Annals* 31 (1908): 639–48.

Ginger, Ray. *Altgeld's America.* New York, 1973.

Goodnow, Frank. "Municipal Home Rule." *Political Science Quarterly* 10 (1895): 1–21.

———. "Municipal Home Rule." *Political Science Quarterly* 21 (1906): 77–90.

———. "The Relation of City and State." *Municipal Affairs* 2 (1898): 689–704.

Gosnell, Harold F. *Machine Politics: Chicago Model.* Chicago, 1937.

Gottfried, Alex. *Boss Cermak of Chicago: A Study of Political Leadership.* Seattle, 1962.

Grant, Bruce. *Fight for a City: The Story of the Union League Club of Chicago and Its Times, 1880–1955.* Chicago, 1955.

Green, Paul M. "Irish Chicago: The Multiethnic Road to Machine Success." In *Ethnic Chicago*, edited by Peter d'A. Jones and Melvin Holli. Grand Rapids, 1981.

———. "The Rise of the Democratic Party in Chicago, 1840–1920." Ph.D. Diss., University of Chicago, 1975.

Griffith, Ernest. *A History of American City Government: The Conspicuous Failure, 1870–1900.* New York, 1974.

———. *A History of American City Government: The Progressive Years, 1900–1920.* New York, 1974.

Grosser, Hugo S. *Chicago: A Review of Its Governmental History, from 1837–1906.* Chicago, 1906.

Haley, Margaret. "My Story." Typescript in Chicago Federation of Teachers Papers at Chicago Historical Society, n.d.

Harris, Carl V. *Political Power in Birmingham, 1871–1921.* Knoxville, 1977.

Harrison, Carter H. "The Regulation of Public Utilities." *The Annals* 57 (1915): 54–61.

———. *Stormy Years: The Autobiography of Carter H. Harrison, Five Times Mayor of Chicago.* Indianapolis, 1935.

Hatton, Augustus R., comp. *Digest of City Charters. Together with Other Statutory and Constitutional Provisions Relating to Cities.* Chicago, 1906.

Hays, Samuel. "The Changing Political Structure of the City in Industrial America." *Journal of Urban History* 1 (1974): 6–38.

———. "The Politics of Reform in Municipal Government in the Progressive Era." *Pacific Northwest Quarterly* 55 (1964): 157–69.

———. "The Social Analysis of American Political History, 1880–1920." *Political Science Quarterly* 80 (1965): 373–94.

Hofstadter, Richard. *The Age of Reform: from Bryan to F.D.R.* New York, 1955.

Holli, Melvin. *Reform in Detroit: Hazen S. Pingree and Urban Politics.* New York, 1969.

"Home Rule Features of the Proposed New Charter." *The City Club Bulletin* 1 (June 1907): 147–56.

Hunter, Robert. *Tenement Conditions in Chicago: A Report by the Investigating Committee of the City Homes Association.* Chicago, 1901.

Illinois Association Opposed to the Extension of Suffrage to Women. *A Protest against the Granting of Municipal Suffrage to Women in the City of Chicago.* 1906 [at Chicago Historical Society].

Jackson, J. C. "The Work of the Anti-Saloon League." *The Annals* 32 (1908): 482–96.

Jones, Peter d'A., and Melvin Holli, eds. *Ethnic Chicago.* Grand Rapids, 1981.

Kantowicz, Edward. *Polish-American Politics in Chicago, 1888–1940.* Chicago, 1975.

Kaplan, Barry J. "Metropolitics, Administrative Reform and Political Theory: The Greater New York City Charter of 1897." *Journal of Urban History* 9 (1983): 165–94.

Karl, Barry D. *Charles E. Merriam and the Study of Politics.* Chicago, 1974.

Katznelson, Ira. *City Trenches: Urban Politics and the Patterning of Class in the United States.* New York, 1981.

King, Hoyt. *Citizen Cole of Chicago.* Chicago, 1931.

———. "The Reform Movement in Chicago." *The Annals* 25 (1905): 235–47.

Kleppner, Paul. *Chicago Divided: The Making of a Black Mayor.* DeKalb, 1985.

———. *The Cross of Culture: A Social Analysis of Midwestern Politics, 1850–1900.* New York, 1970.

Komons, Nick A. "Chicago, 1893–1907: The Politics of Reform." Ph.D. Diss., George Washington University, 1961.

Lepawsky, Albert. *Home Rule for Metropolitan Chicago.* Chicago, 1932.

McBain, Howard L. "The Doctrine of an Inherent Right to Self-Government." *Columbia Law Review* 16 (1916): 299–322.

McCarthy, Kathleen. *Noblesse Oblige: Charity and Cultural Philanthropy in Chicago, 1849–1929.* Chicago, 1982.

McCarthy, Michael P. "Businessmen and Professionals in Municipal Reform: The Chicago Experience, 1887–1920." Ph.D. Diss., Northwestern University, 1970.

———. "The New Metropolis: Chicago, The Annexation Movement, and Progressive Reform." In *The Age of Urban Reform: New Perspec-*

tives on the Progressive Era, edited by Michael Ebner and Eugene Tobin. Port Washington, 1977.

———. "On Bosses, Reformers, and Urban Growth: Some Suggestions for a Political Typology of American Cities." *Journal of Urban History* 4 (1977): 29–38.

———. "Prelude to Armageddon: Charles E. Merriam and the Chicago Mayoral Campaign of 1911." *Journal of the Illinois State Historical Society* 67 (1974): 505–18.

McKay, John P. *Tramways and Trolleys: The Rise of Urban Transport in Europe*. Princeton, 1976.

Maltbie, Milo R. "City-made Charters." *Yale Review* 13 (1905): 380–407.

Mayer, Harold, and Richard Wade. *Chicago: Growth of a Metropolis*. Chicago, 1969.

Merriam, Charles E. "The Case for Home Rule." *The Annals* 57 (1915): 170–74.

———. *Chicago: A More Intimate View of Urban Politics*. New York, 1929.

———. "Chicago Charter Convention." *American Political Science Review* 2 (1907): 1–14.

———. "Home Rule in Chicago's New Charter." The *Voter* (1907): 24–32.

———. *Report of an Investigation of the Municipal Revenues of Chicago*. Chicago, 1906.

Merriam, Robert E., and Norman Elken. *The Charters of Chicago: A Summary*. Chicago, 1952.

Miller, Richard G. "Fort Worth and the Progressive Era: The Movement for Charter Revision, 1899–1907." In *Essays on Urban America*, edited by Margaret F. Morris and Elliott West. Austin, 1975.

Munro, William. *A Bibliography of Municipal Government in the United States*. Cambridge, 1913.

Nord, David. "The Experts Versus the Experts: Conflicting Philosophies of Municipal Utility Regulation in the Progressive Era." *Wisconsin Magazine of History* 58 (1974–75): 219–36.

———. "The Public Community: The Urbanization of Journalism in Chicago." *Journal of Urban History* 11 (1985): 411–38.

Oberholtzer, Ellis P. "Home Rule for Our American Cities." *The Annals* 3 (1892–93): 736–63.

Parrington, Vernon L. *Main Currents of American Thought*. New York, 1927–1930.

Pease, Otis A. "Urban Reformers in the Progressive Era: A Reassessment." *Pacific Northwest Quarterly* 62 (April 1971): 49–58.

Philip, William B. "Chicago and the Downstate: A Study of Their Conflicts, 1870–1934." Ph.D. Diss., University of Chicago, 1940.

Philpott, Thomas Lee. *The Slum and the Ghetto: Neighborhood Deterioration and Middle-Class Reform, Chicago, 1880–1930.* New York, 1978.

Pierce, Bessie L. *As Others See Chicago: Impressions of Visitors, 1673–1933.* Chicago, 1933.

———. *History of Chicago.* Vol. 3, *The Rise of a Modern City, 1871–1893.* Chicago, 1957.

Platt, Harold L. "City-Building and Progressive Reform: The Modernization of an Urban Polity, Houston, 1892–1905." In *The Age of Urban Reform: New Perspectives on the Progressive Era*, edited by Michael Ebner and Eugene Tobin. Port Washington, 1977.

———. *City Building in the New South: The Growth of Public Services in Houston, Texas, 1830–1910.* Philadelphia, 1983.

"Political Features of the Proposed City Charter." The City Club *Bulletin* 1 (July 1907): 165–73.

Post, Louis F. "Living a Long Life Over." Typescript in Louis F. Post Papers, box no. 4, Library of Congress, n.d.

Prichard, Frank P. "The Study of the Science of Municipal Government." *The Annals* 2 (1891–92): 450–57.

"Report of the Permanent Charter Commission to the City Council." *Journal of the Proceedings of the Chicago City Council* (1915): 1126–28.

"Revenue Provisions of the Proposed New Charter." The City Club *Bulletin* 1 (June 1907): 157–63.

Rice, Bradley. "The Galveston Plan of City Government by Commission: The Birth of a Progressive Idea." *Southwestern Historical Quarterly* 73 (1975): 367–408.

Schiesl, Martin J. *The Politics of Efficiency: Municipal Administration and Reform in America, 1880–1920.* Berkeley, 1977.

———. "Progressive Reform in Los Angeles under Mayor Alexander, 1909–1913." *California Historical Quarterly* 54 (1975): 37–56.

Sikes, George. "Chicago's New Mayor." *American Monthly Review of Reviews* (1907): 585–88.

———. "How Chicago Is Winning Good Government." *Proceedings of the Providence Conference for Good City Goverment and the Thir-*

teenth Annual Meeting of the National Municipal League. National Municipal League, 1907.

Sparling, Samuel E. *Municipal History and Present Organization of the City of Chicago*. Madison, 1898.

Spear, Allan H. *Black Chicago: The Making of a Negro Ghetto, 1890–1920*. Chicago, 1967.

Steffens, Lincoln. *The Shame of the Cities*. New York, 1902.

Sunny, B. E. *The Proposed Amendment to the Constitution of Illinois and a New Charter for Chicago*. 1904 [at Chicago Historical Society].

Sutherland, Douglas. *Fifty Years on the Civic Front: A History of the Civic Federation*. Chicago, 1943.

Tarr, Joel A. *A Study in Boss Politics: William Lorimer of Chicago*. Urbana, 1971.

———. "William Kent to Lincoln Steffens: Origins of Progressive Reform in Chicago." *Mid-America* (1965): 48–57.

Teaford, Jon C. *The Twentieth-Century American City: Problem, Promise and Reality*. Baltimore, 1986.

Thelen, David P. "Social Tensions and the Origins of Progressivism." *Journal of American History* 56 (1968): 323–41.

Tompkins, C. David. "John Peter Altgeld as a Candidate for Mayor of Chicago in 1899." *Journal of the Illinois State Historical Society* 56 (1963): 654–76.

Truman, David B. *The Governmental Process: Political Interests and Public Opinion*. New York, 1971.

United Societies for Local Self-Government. *Home Rule: The Truth about the Sunday Question*. 1907 [at Chicago Historical Society].

———. *Seven Reasons to Vote against the Charter*. 1907 [printed in Illinois *Staats-Zeitung*]

Urban, Wayne. "Progressive Education in the Urban South: Reform of the Atlanta Schools, 1914–1918." In *The Age of Urban Reform: New Perspectives on the Progressive Era*, edited by Michael Ebner and Eugene Tobin. Port Washington, 1977.

Weber, Adna F. *The Growth of Cities in the Nineteenth Century*. New York, 1899.

Weinstein, James. "Organized Business and the City Commission and Manager Movements." *Journal of Southern History* 28 (1962): 166–82.

Wendt, Lloyd, and Herman Kogan. *Bosses in Lusty Chicago*. Bloomington, 1943.

Wheeler, Adade, and Marlene Wortman. *The Roads They Made: Women in Illinois History.* Chicago, 1977.

Wiebe, Robert H. *Businessmen and Reform: A Study of the Progressive Movement.* Cambridge, 1962.

———. *The Search for Order, 1877–1920.* New York, 1967.

Woodruff, Clinton R. "A Freer City—A Plea for Municipal Home Rule." *Yale Review* 12 (1904): 360–71.

Yearley, Clifton K. *The Money Machines: The Breakdown and Reform of Governmental and Party Finance in the North, 1860–1920.* Albany, 1970.

INDEX

Addams, Jane, ix, 36, 37, 40–41; and municipal suffrage for women, 84, 125
Allen Bill, 43
Altgeld, John P., 43–44; and Haymarket pardons, 31; and Pullman strike, 32; as 1899 mayoral candidate, 43–44
Annexation movement, 13, 14–16; and temperance, 15–16, 33
Anti-Saloon League, 33, 72, 106
Armour, Philip, 16, 31
Atlanta, 82

Bennett, Frank I., 73, 94, 116, 117
Berry, Orville, 106, 132, 133
Blacks, in Chicago, 19; representation of, in charter convention, 61
Board of Education (Chicago), 98, 99, 104, 107–9, 156, 159, 160. *See also* Public school reform
Bonfield, John "Black Jack," 29, 30
Bosses, versus reformers, x, 127–28
Boston, 19, 22, 64–65
Bowen, Louise DeKoven, 124
Business efficiency, 69; and pub-

lic school reform, 78–79, 81–82, 103–4, 108–9, 149
Businessmen, 29, 39, 43; and annexation, 16, 31–32; and Haymarket, 30–32; and municipal ownership, 74, 91, 92, 101, 102; and Pullman strike, 3; and reform, 49, 50, 51, 55–56, 58, 61, 69, 116–17, 121–22, 139–40, 148
Busse, Fred A., 74, 99–100, 101, 102, 103, 105, 122, 123, 134; and board of education, 104, 107–9; as charter supporter, 99, 100, 105, 134; support of, for charter bills (1909), 145; and traction reform, 102, 103; and United Societies for Local Self-Government, 105, 132

Case studies of urban reform, 3–4
Centralization, 9, 64–65, 67
Central Labor Union, 29, 30
Cermak, Anton J., 144, 145, 153, 156; and United Societies for Local Self-Government, 144, 151
Charter (1907), 95–97; before the General Assembly, 105–7; as a home-rule document, 72,

MAUREEN A. FLANAGAN received her Ph.D. in 1981 from Loyola University of Chicago and is currently a departmental associate in the Department of History at Northwestern University. She has published articles on Chicago's political history in the *Journal of Urban History* and the *Journal of the Illinois State Historical Society.* Her article on Fred Busse, mayor during the charter reform movement, appeared in *The Mayors: The Chicago Political Tradition*, edited by Paul Green and Melvin Holli (Southern Illinois University Press, 1987).